Qual.

PURIFICATION

AN ILLUSTRATED ANSWER TO DRUGS

L. RON HUBBARD

PURIFICATION

AN ILLUSTRATED ANSWER TO DRUGS

Bridge PUBLICATIONS, INC.

A HUBBARD PUBLICATION

Published in the USA by
Bridge Publications, Inc.
4751 Fountain Avenue
Los Angeles, California 90029

ISBN 0-88404-567-6

Published in all other countries by
NEW ERA Publications International, ApS
Store Kongensgade 55
1264 Copenhagen K, Denmark

ISBN 87-7336-744-3

This book is part of the works of L. Ron Hubbard, who developed *Scientology®* applied religious philosophy. It is presented to the reader as a record of observations and research into the nature of the human mind and spirit, and not as a statement of claims made by the author. The benefits and goals of Scientology can be attained only by the dedicated efforts of the reader.

The *Purification* program cannot be construed as a recommendation of medical treatment or medication and it is not professed as a physical handling for bodies nor is any claim made to that effect. There are no medical recommendations or claims for the *Purification* program or for any of the vitamin or mineral regimens described in this book.

No individual should undertake the *Purification* program or any of its regimens without first consulting and obtaining the informed approval of a licensed medical practitioner. The author makes no warranties or representation as to the effectiveness of the *Purification* program.

Printed in the United States of America

IMPORTANT NOTE

In reading this book, be very certain you never go past a word you do not fully understand.

The only reason a person gives up a study or becomes confused or unable to learn is because he or she has gone past a word that was not understood.

The confusion or inability to grasp or learn comes AFTER a word that the person did not have defined and understood.

Have you ever had the experience of coming to the end of a page and realizing you didn't know what you had read? Well, somewhere earlier on that page you went past a word that you had no definition for or an incorrect definition for.

Here's an example. "It was found that when the crepuscule arrived the children were quieter and when it was not present, they were much livelier." You see what happens. You think you don't understand the whole idea, but the inability to understand came entirely from the one word you could not define, *crepuscule,* which means twilight or darkness.

It may not only be the new and unusual words that you will have to look up. Some commonly used words can often be misdefined and so cause confusion.

This datum about not going past an undefined word is the most important fact in the whole subject of study. Every subject you have taken up and abandoned had its words which you failed to get defined.

Therefore, in studying this book be very, very certain you never go past a word you do not fully understand. If the material becomes confusing or you can't seem to grasp it, there will be a word just earlier that you have not understood. Don't go any further, but go back to BEFORE you got into difficulty, find the misunderstood word and get it defined.

A DOCTOR'S EVALUATION OF THE PURIFICATION PROGRAM

by Gene Denk
Bachelor of Science, Doctor of Medicine

"An Evaluation of a Detoxification Program for Long-Term Stored Chemicals" is the title of a paper first published in 1981 and then appearing in Medical Hypothesis *September 1982 by myself in concert with two colleagues: Megan Shields, M.D. and Steven Burton, M.D.*

This paper was the result of extensive study and testing of the Purification program developed by L. Ron Hubbard. The following are excerpts from the publication outlining some of our findings:

> The purpose of this current study is to evaluate and document clinically observed physical or psychological changes that occur upon conclusion of the Purification program. In addition to clinical evaluations, psychological tests and standard blood chemistry were performed.
>
> One hundred and three volunteers were selected to represent varying degrees of drug usage. California guidelines for human experimentation were followed, and informed consent obtained from all participants. Volunteers were accepted on a first-application-received basis, covering the spectrum from heavy (i.e., frequent heroin usage, hallucinogenics, frequent or severe use of medical drugs) to no drug usage. Most of the participants were from the Hollywood population at large and twenty were from Narconon Los Angeles, a local drug rehabilitation center. The volunteers were interviewed and demographic data (statistical data showing average age, income, education, etc.) was collected. This data was used to ensure a cross-section of drug users and of the general population were included in the study.
>
> A large variety of incidents occurred, as individuals progressed through the program, which were suggestive of drugs or chemicals being released from the body. There were reports of brief, full-blown "LSD trips" with hallucinations; some participants who had had ether (a colorless, sweet-smelling liquid used as an anesthetic) would smell like ether in the sauna; old injuries would flare up with swelling or redness along surgery

lines and then resolve over a few days. The flushing that followed ingestion of niacin frequently would occur along lines of bathing suits or old sunburns; this would diminish over a few days then reoccur in a different pattern. It was not unusual to have a person reexperience the physical condition associated with taking a certain drug or anesthetic. For instance, one patient complained of onset of mild pain in the lower right quarter of the body, nausea, light-headedness and reddening of an old appendix scar line. This reoccurred the next two days at lessening severity and then was gone in three days.

The program appears safe as long as done under the care of a physician. The exercise and sauna are tolerated very well as long as they are begun on a gradient. As with any major physical exercise program, however, general physical condition and physical health need to be monitored. The authors feel this program is unadvisable for any person with heart disease or any other major physical disabilities unless directly done under the supervision of a physician who is willing to work out a specific exercise, sauna and vitamin program for the patient.

Since the first publication of the above findings, tens of thousands of people have successfully undergone the Purification program, and the theories presented in this book are gaining increasing acceptance among medical doctors and scientists.

Dr. Denk graduated Bachelor of Science from University of Michigan and Doctor of Medicine at University of Washington at Seattle. He maintains a private practice in Los Angeles.

PREFACE

This book presents material on the Purification program, a procedure researched and developed, in view of the current environmental and drug scene, to put the mental and spiritual help available in Dianetics and Scientology processing within the reach of every individual.

The Purification program does not supplant technology developed and in use especially in Narconon drug rehabilitation centers for persons currently on drugs and apt to experience withdrawal symptoms when taken off them. The program would be begun only after such technology was applied.

We are not concerned with handling bodies with the Purification program. Our concern is freeing the individual up spiritually. The only dosages recommended are those classified as food. There are no medical recommendations or claims for it. The only claim is future spiritual improvement.

This data is released as a record of researches and results noted. It cannot be construed as a recommendation of medical treatment or medication and it is undertaken or delivered by anyone on his own responsibility. I receive no percentage of fees for administering this program, and my development of it is a contribution and gift to my friends.

L. Ron Hubbard

PURIFICATION
PROGRAM

It's a drug-ridden world—

but there is *hope* for changing this—
on the Purification program.

You pay a lot for drugs
whether you have money . . .

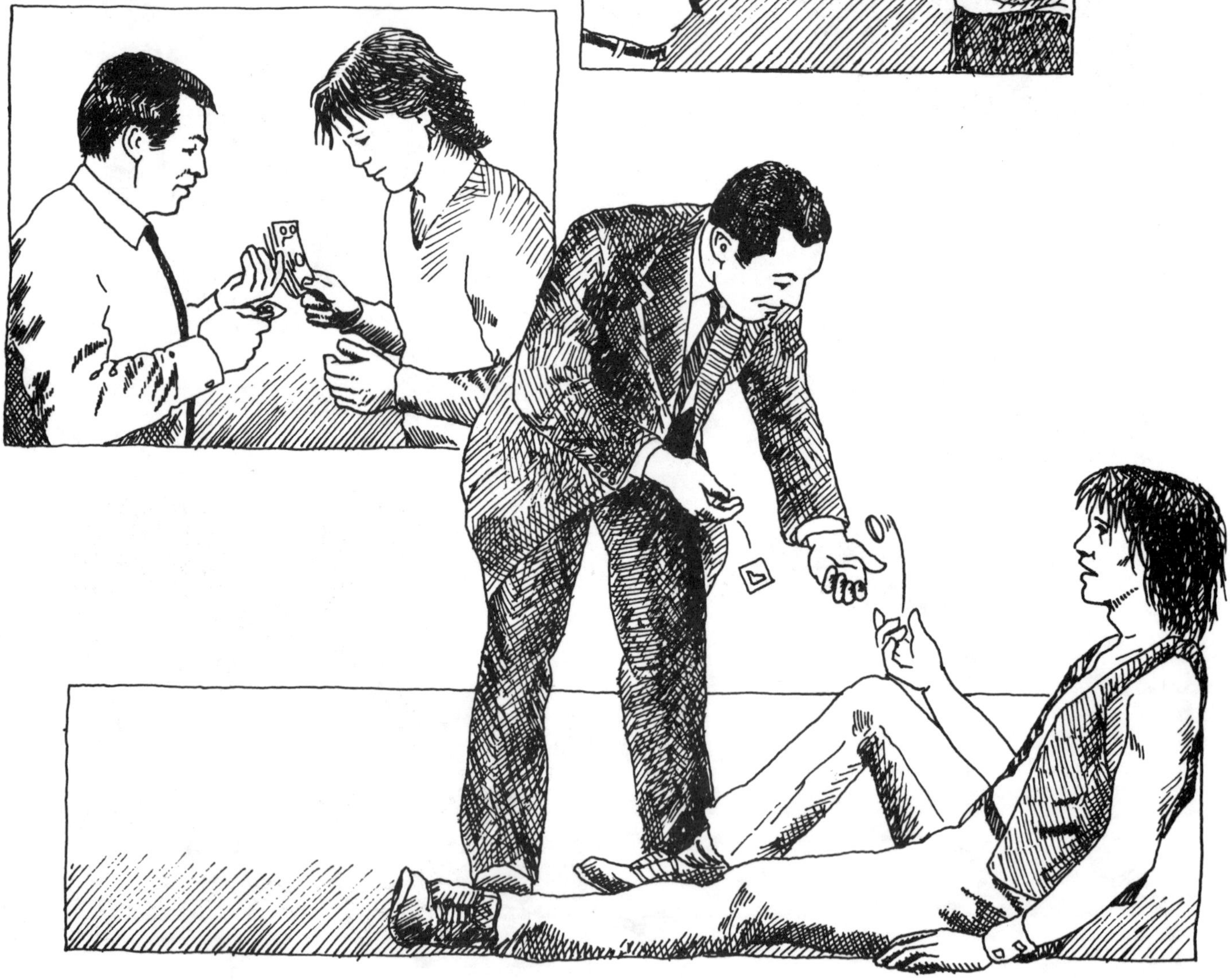

"On drugs, I didn't want to do much of anything—except force myself to keep a job to support my drug habit. I was in a trap which was controlling me." —R.C.K.

. . . or whether you don't have it.

"I was a slave to drugs and alcohol." —R.C.K.

Even after coming off drugs you can wind up paying

for years . . .

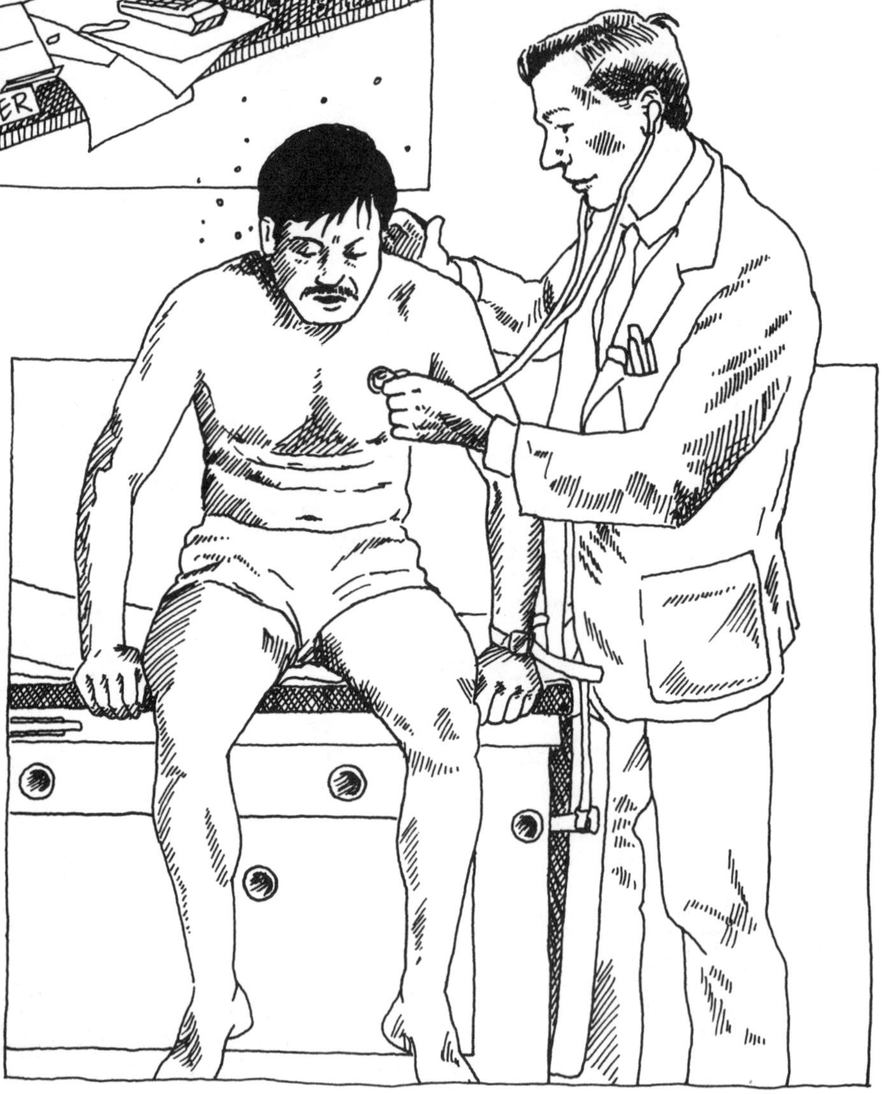

> **"That 'wooden feeling' started when I started taking drugs and I don't remember having it before drugs."**
> **—L.M.**

. . . and years.

"For the last nine years of my life I've suffered from the side effects of having used drugs." —D.B.

But there is HELP available on the Purification program.

In the 1970s, working with cases of individuals who had been drug users, and in a study of their physical symptoms and behavioral patterns, I made a startling discovery.

LSD can lodge in the body tissues—mainly the fatty tissues—and stay there for years and years after a person has taken it.

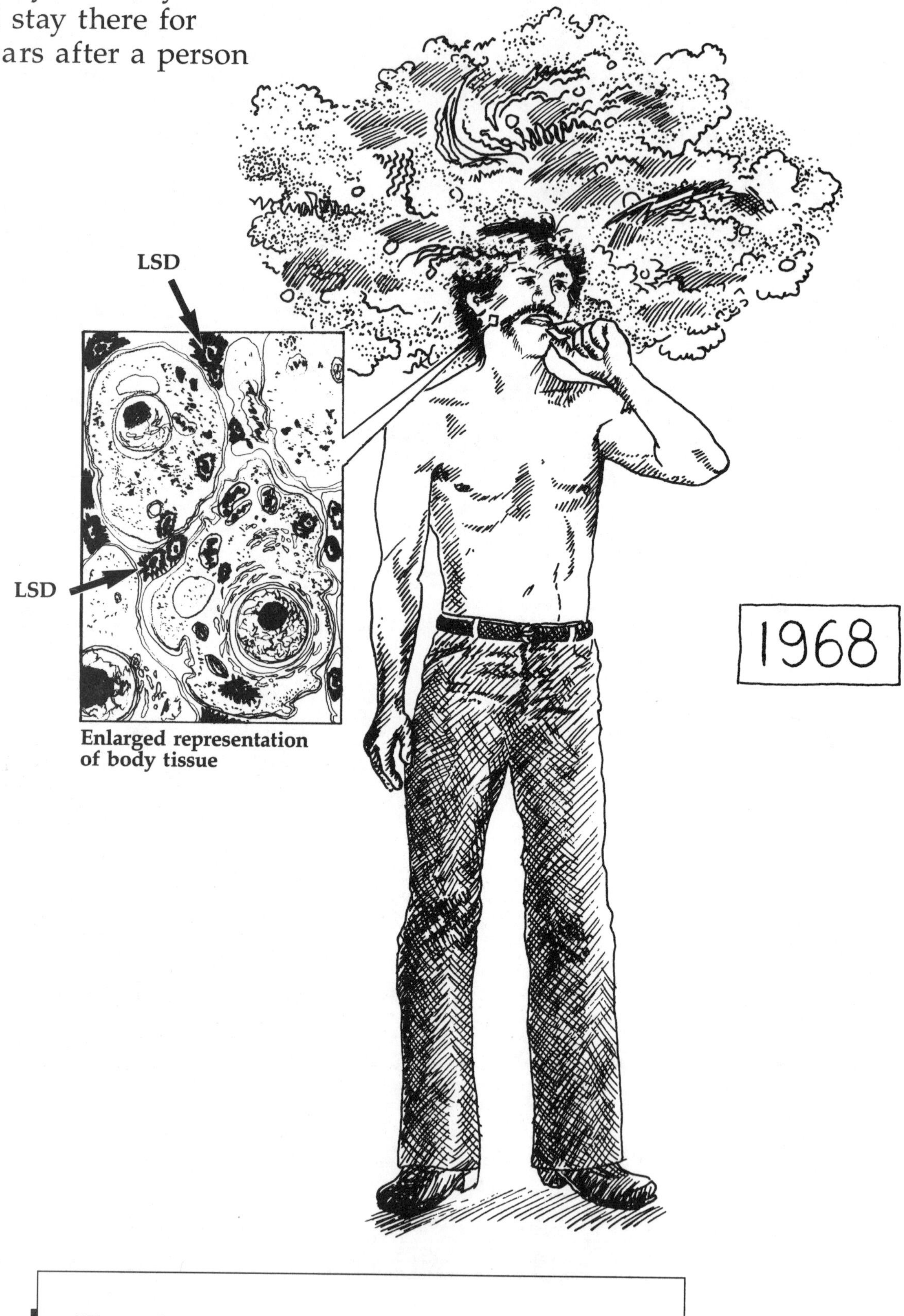

Enlarged representation of body tissue

"Even after coming off drugs, there were times I felt high—a floating feeling which reminded me of a time I was high on pot. Another time I felt a little like nausea, like when I was drunk on rum." —A.D.

It can go into action *years* later, giving the person unpredictable "trips"—as if he had just taken more LSD.

Enlarged representation of body tissue

"Even after coming off drugs, I experienced visual patterns and distortions which I had previously encountered with LSD." —D.K.

Further research has now shown that other drugs—heroin, cocaine, angel dust, mescaline, peyote, marijuana—to name a few—can also lodge in the system . . .

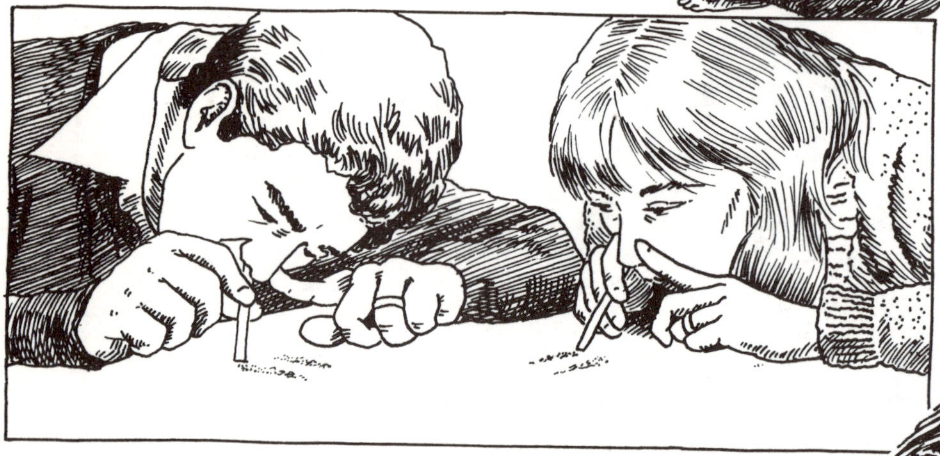

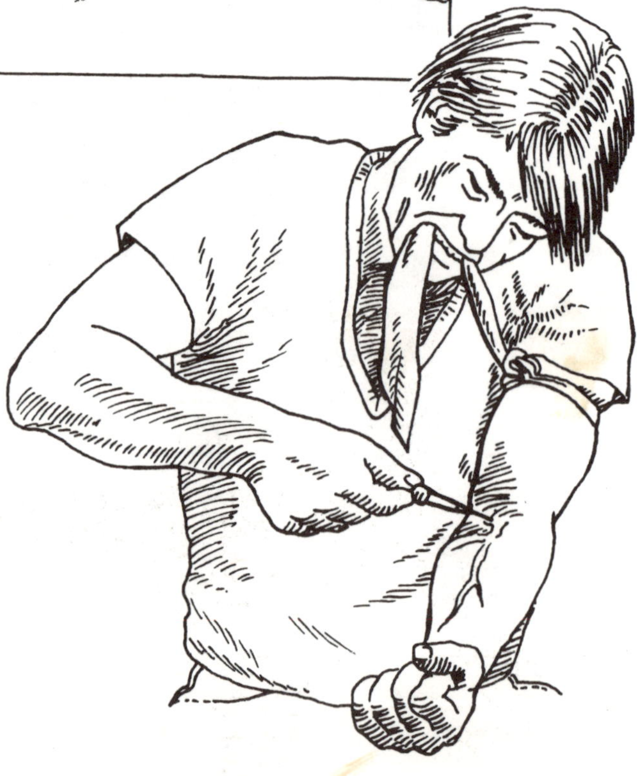

and later get triggered into action or "reactivated"—as if the person had just taken more of the drug.

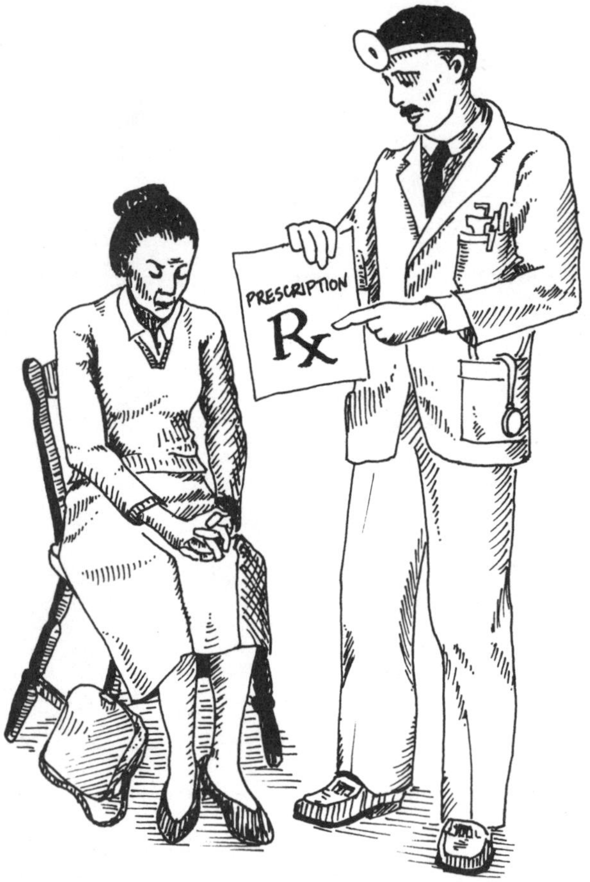

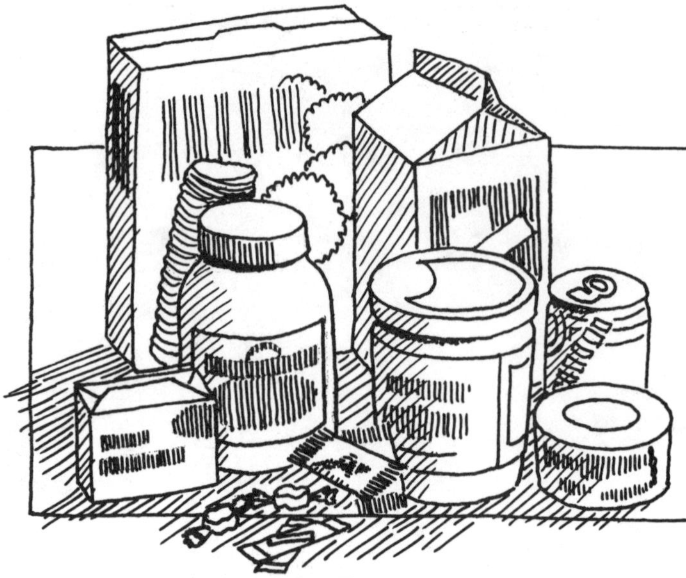

It appears that medicinal drugs, food preservatives, tranquilizers . . .

pesticides,
chemical wastes . . .

radiation

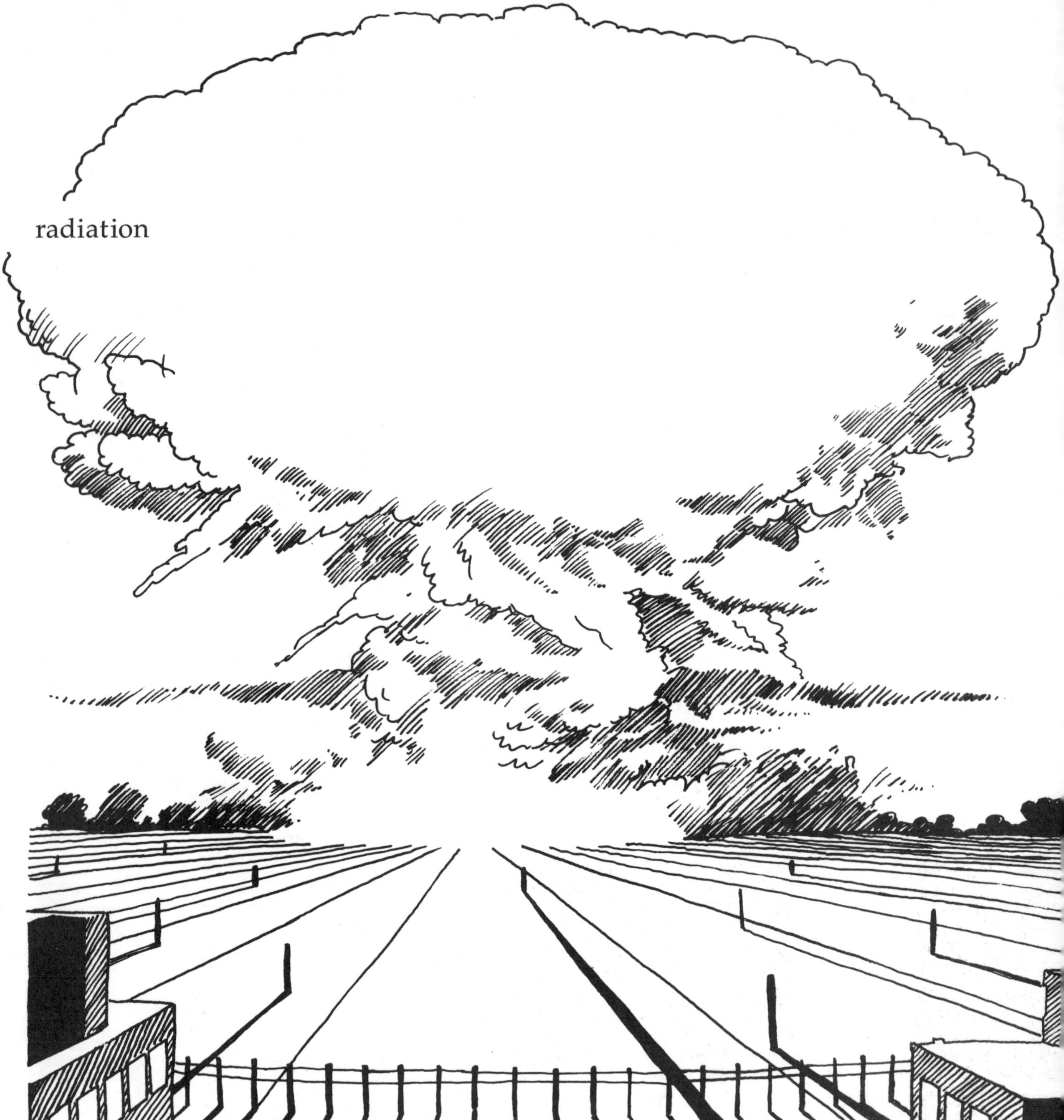

"Prior to starting the Purification program, I had a history of moderately heavy radiation exposure. This consisted of long periods of sun exposure through childhood and college and frequent X-ray exposure from working around X-ray machines with patients for some seven-odd years. During the program I had several episodes of extreme flush, splotchy rashes accompanied by nausea and a very solid, wooden feeling. From my viewpoint as a physician, this raises several questions on what effects low-grade radiation of different types over a lifetime can have on a being or his body—probably more significant than is currently recognized." —G.D.

and other toxic substances

can also get caught up in the tissues and accumulate there—causing later reactions.

Two or three years after my announcement of the discovery that drug residues can lodge in the system, medical experts doing autopsies also found this to be true.

This discovery is a tremendous step forward in handling drugs and other toxic elements and their effects.

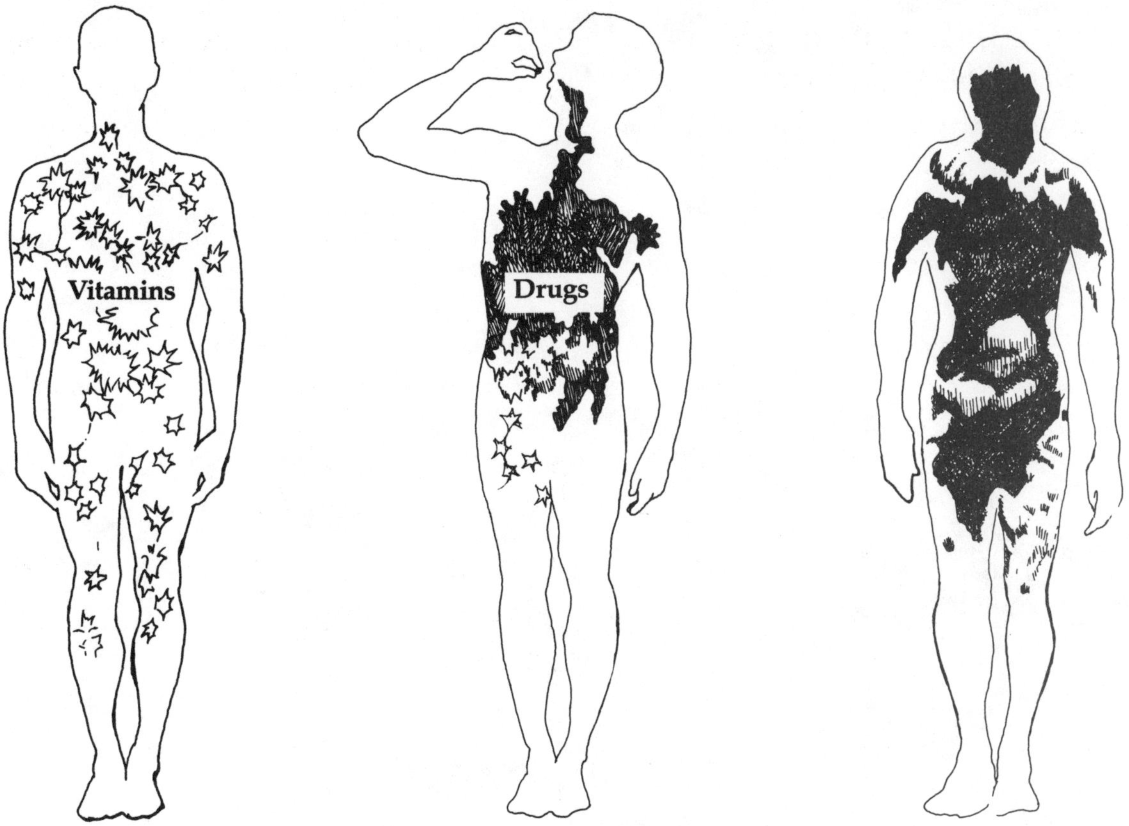

Drugs are essentially poisons. Drug deposits stored in the tissues take their toll.

They eat up the body's store of vitamins and minerals and can create nutritional deficiencies.

"After coming off drugs I was sick a lot with stomach-aches, tired all the time and would sometimes crave drugs." —K.B.

Even after coming off drugs the person has *mental* pictures of drugs and drug experiences.

As long as actual toxic substances are locked in the body they can "restimulate" (reactivate) these pictures.

Drugs and chemical deposits can make it difficult to think clearly. They can make the person appear dull or stupid.

When these deposits are "triggered" they can cause one to "hallucinate." (That means to see things which aren't there.)

"With the reactions I had, it was scary to realize I still had drugs in my body." —F.R.

These poisons that are trapped in the body can change one's attitude toward life—and toward others.

They can stop any personal improvement or forward progress. They can prevent a person from getting mental or spiritual help.

> **"Being an alcoholic and drug user over the past ten years, I was basically thinking and acting like, 'What's the use?' " —R.C.**

Drugs and drug deposits can be costly. The cost can be in terms of money,

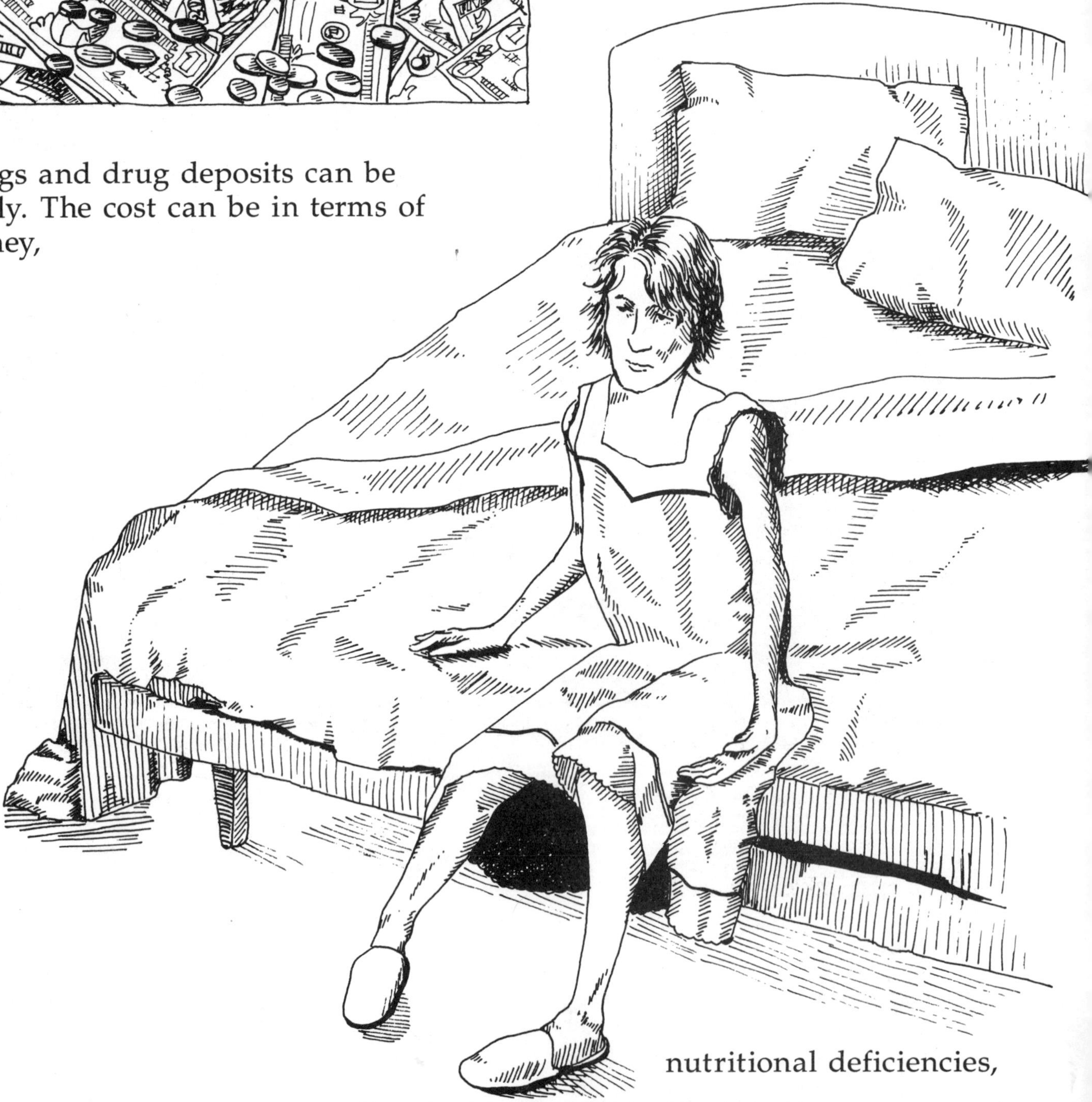

nutritional deficiencies,

bad health,

hopelessness,

broken relationships,

failures

and other grim effects— but . . .

the Purification program can help to release and flush out these harmful deposits.

> **"I've done a lot of drugs throughout the last five years. Now, after the Purification program, my body feels clean and I have a clear head for once in my life. I can really feel the difference and it's great!" —R.H.**

Before the development of the Purification program, nothing had been found that would actually move or dislodge drug residues from the tissues.

For those who have had drugs of any kind, there is NO OTHER RESCUE that is effective.

"The Purification program was the beginning of a new life for me." —D.S.

Now there is *hope* with the Purification program. This is a program which can change the face of society!

"Earlier I had never doubted my abilities, but drugs changed that. I started giving up and got tired of life. I became destructive. Now, after the Purification program, I have my old point of view back, but with a difference—I can play a much bigger game!" —A.D.

ENROLL ON THE PURIFICATION PROGRAM.

IT COULD CHANGE YOUR LIFE!

"After completing the Purification program I have much more energy and the future looks bright and positive." —C.J.

First you will be sent to a medical doctor for an examination and written medical approval to do the program.

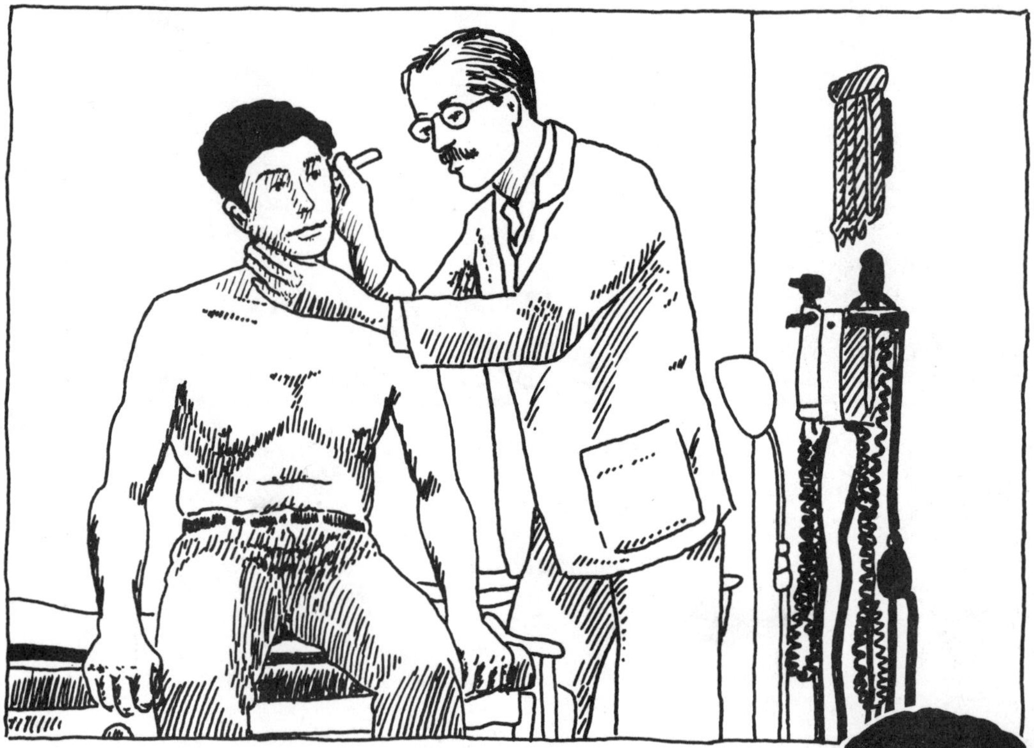

Next you take some simple tests.

Each step of the Purification program is important. Each step must be done exactly as given.

This program can be strenuous and should not be undertaken by anyone who has a weak heart or who is anemic.

The program is best done under the guidance of those persons trained and qualified in supervising it. Each step should be very closely supervised and controlled. Scientology organizations around the world are fully set up to deliver the Purification program, with technical personnel thoroughly trained in the exact application and supervision of the program.

For people with heart conditions, kidney conditions, anemia or high blood pressure, a much lighter program would be worked out with a medical doctor.

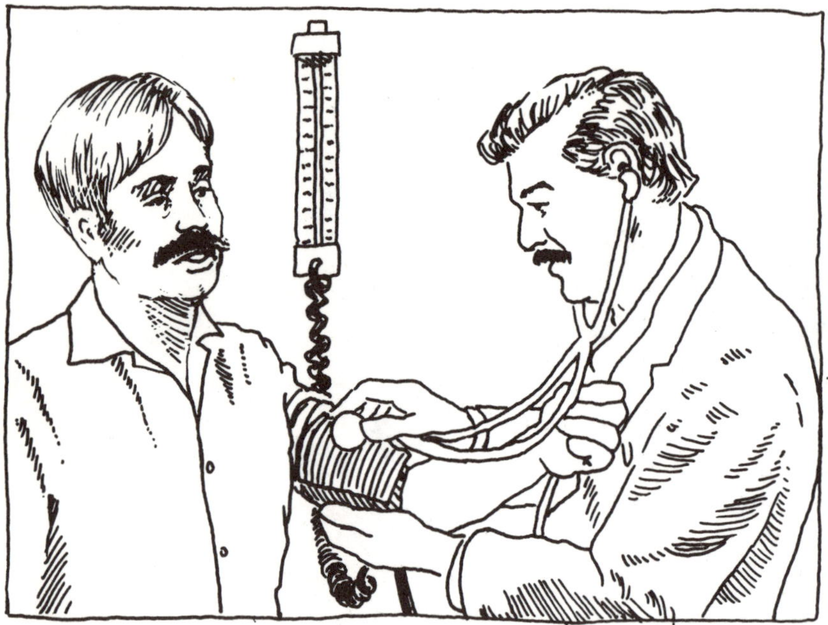

The Administrator of the Purification program will help you with any questions you may have. Agree to follow the steps of the program exactly, through to its completion.

How long does the Purification program take? On a standard schedule of five hours per day on the program, most people go through it in two to three weeks.

"After two weeks on the program, each cigarette I had tasted like the first one I ever had—like chemicals, tar and nicotine. I went from one to two packs a day to zero packs without even trying. I didn't feel a physical need to smoke, or want to. All those accumulations felt gone from my body." —M.H.

A properly ordered personal schedule is worked out for you to follow daily.

It will include:

- exercise and sauna (Most people do best on five hours combined running and sauna. Most of this time is spent in the sauna.),

- proper nutrition, including vegetables, vitamins and minerals in specified amounts

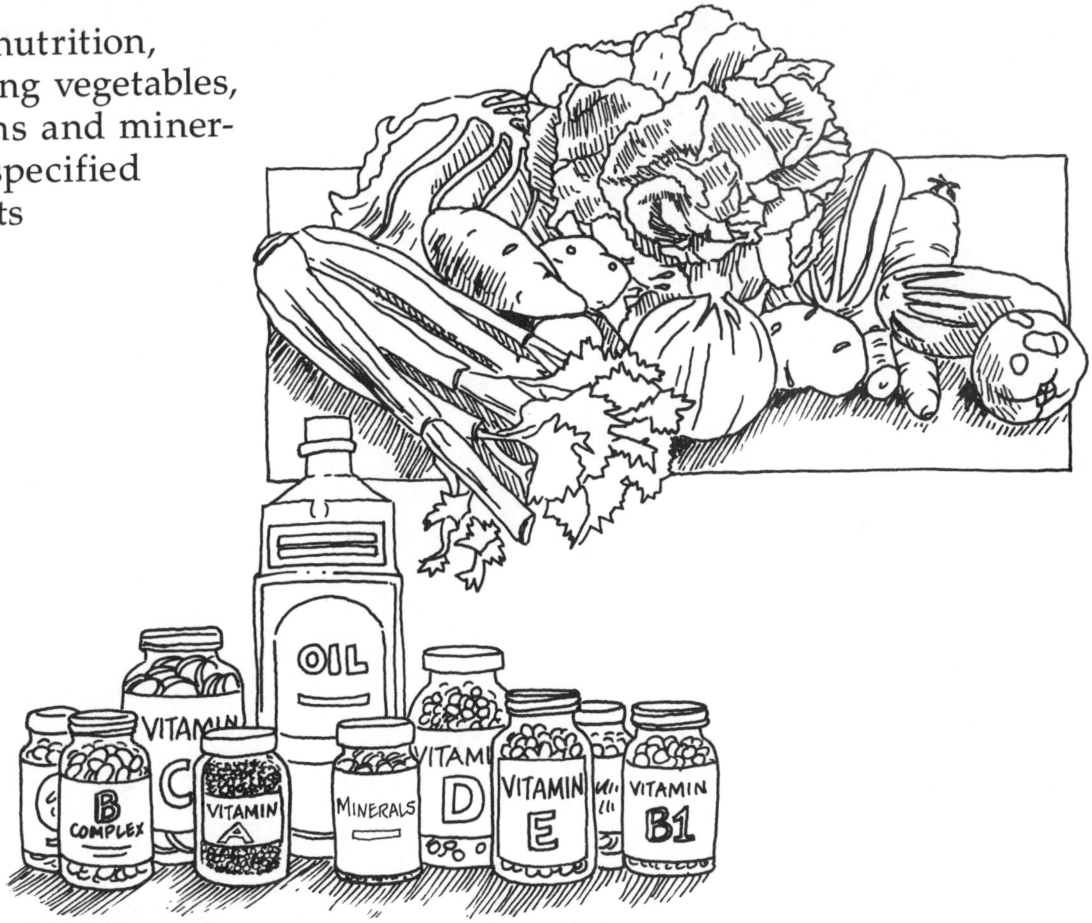

- and a good night's sleep every night.

You work on the program every day under the close supervision of the Purification Program Administrator.

> **"I don't think I ever experienced so many changes in such a concentrated period of time before. One day in the sauna I could feel my legs and feet which had obviously been 'shut off' for many years! On the Purification program I ran out things I didn't even know were in my body." —P.I.**

Special instructions are relayed to you daily from the Program Case Supervisor, and the Administrator checks and reports on your progress.

The first action is running.
Always run with another person.
Running is taken on a gradient—
after starting you will work up to
at least one-half hour daily.

"I don't get tired in the middle of the day anymore. I feel alive, more alive than I've ever felt. The Purification program was fantastic." —D.D.

Running gets the blood circulating faster and the system warmed up.

The blood circulation then goes deeper into the tissues where the harmful deposits are trapped.

This can help to loosen these deposits.

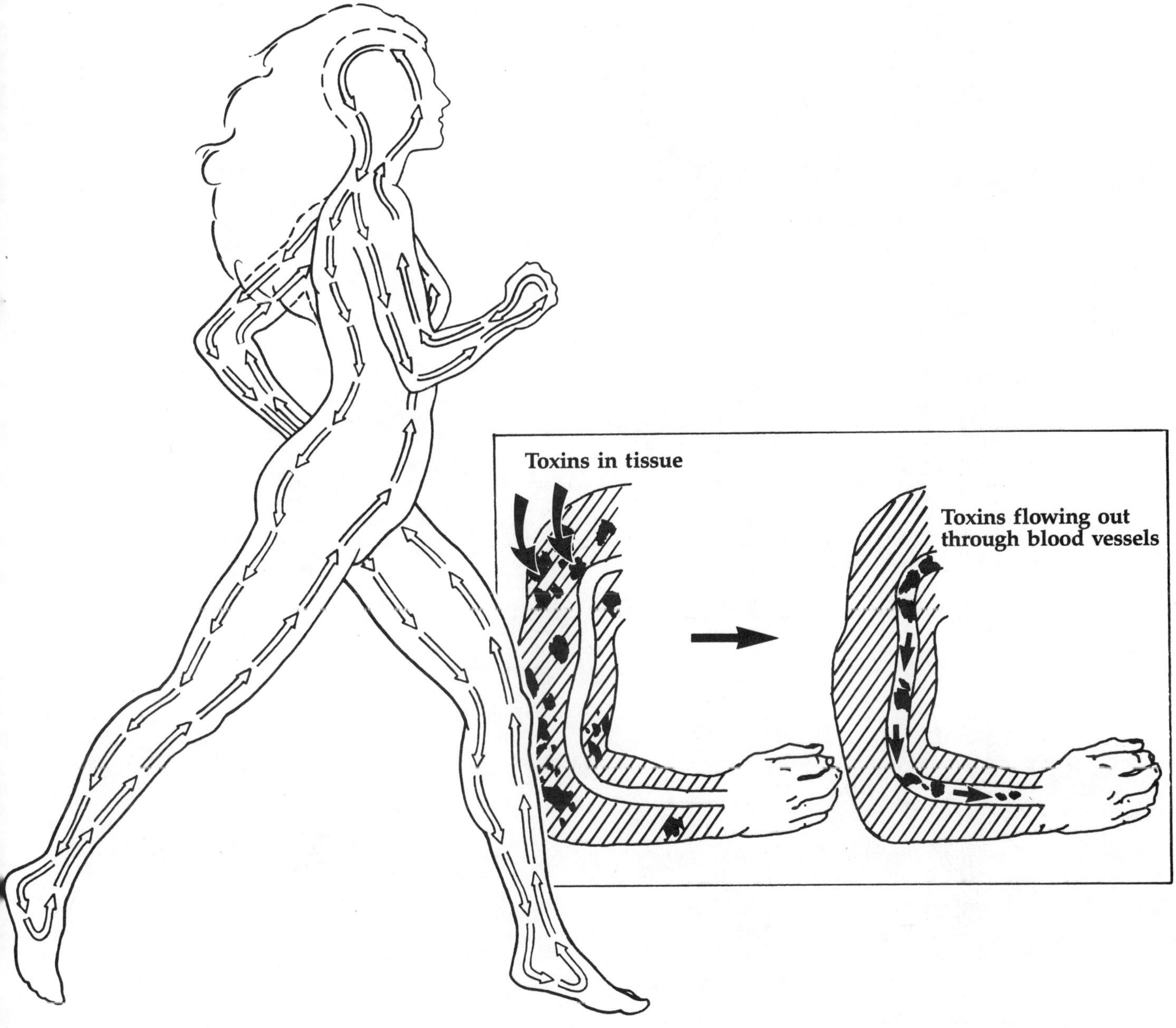

> **"I used to get 'clouds' in my head and feel not completely able to confront things. Now I can see so clearly it's wonderful. This Purification program is incredible!" —S.E.**

The second action immediately following the running is the sauna. Sweating in the sauna is one of the actions of this program that helps release the drug residuals from the system.

"In the sauna I noticed a metallic taste in my mouth, a typical LSD phenomenon which I knew well. I was surprised, as the last time I had taken LSD was four years before. This eventually vanished as I did the program and it has not recurred." —D.R.

A person beginning the program starts at a lower temperature in the sauna and works up to a higher temperature. (Sauna temperatures can range from 140 degrees to 180 degrees F.)

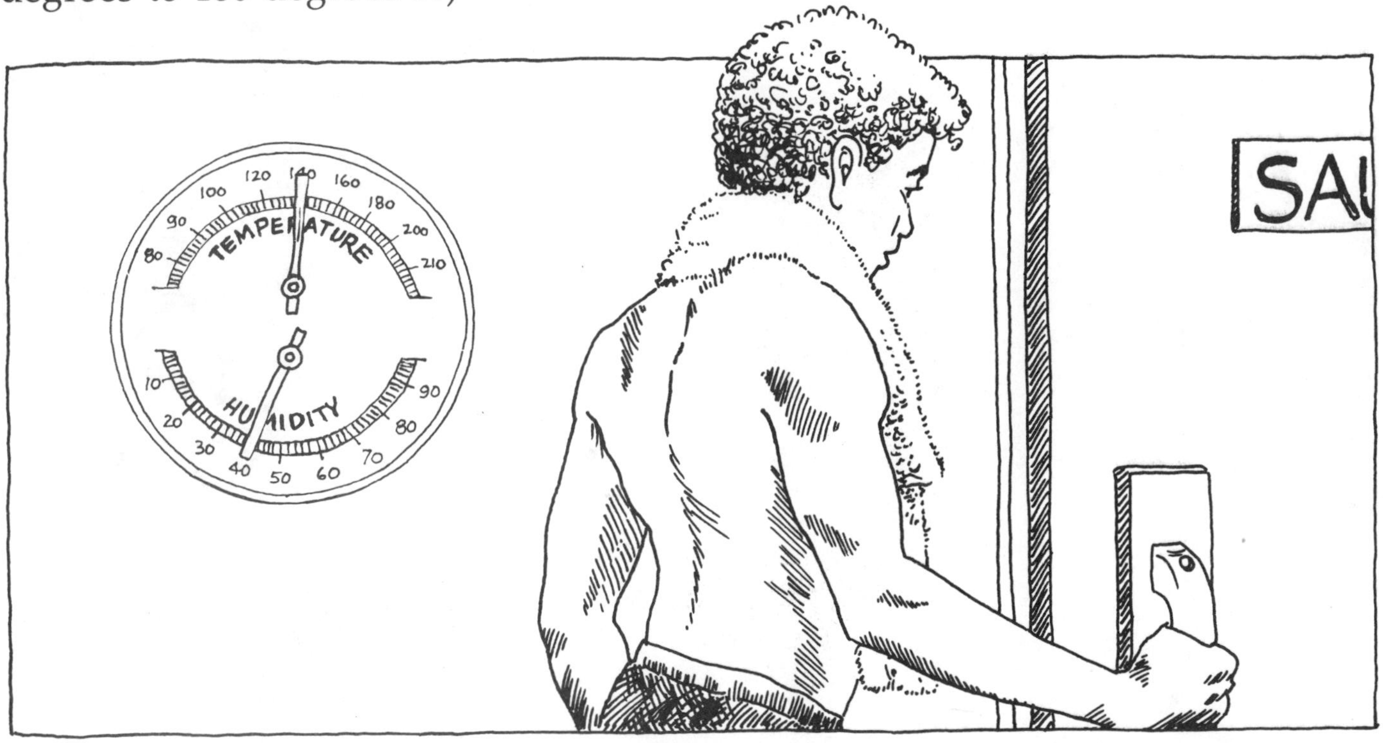

One always does the sauna with another person and works up to 4 or 4½ hours daily in the sauna.

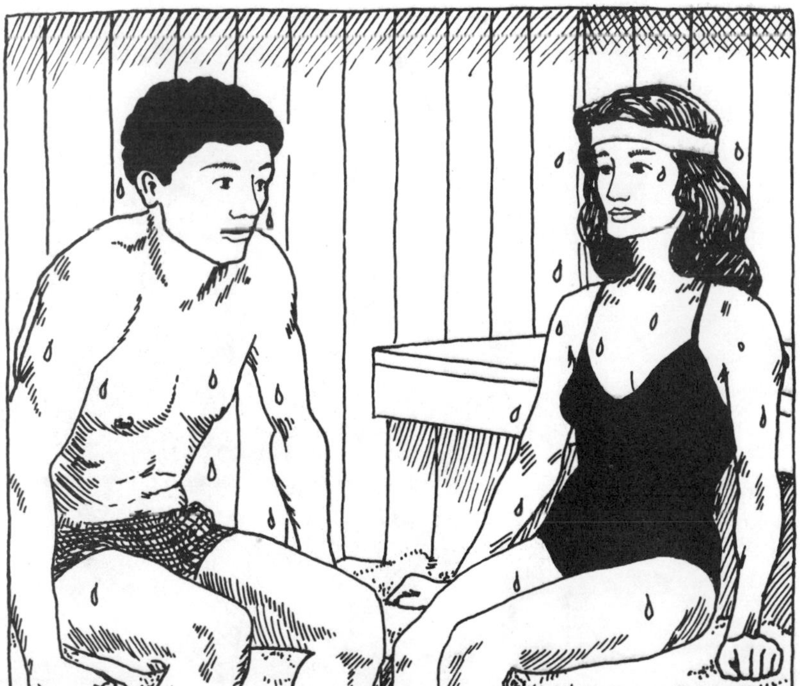

One drinks plenty of liquids to replace liquids lost in sweating. Liquids also help in flushing out the system.

Salt and potassium are always near the sauna because these minerals are lost in sweating and need to be replaced.

If one gets too hot in the sauna, one goes outside and cools off

or takes a cool shower,

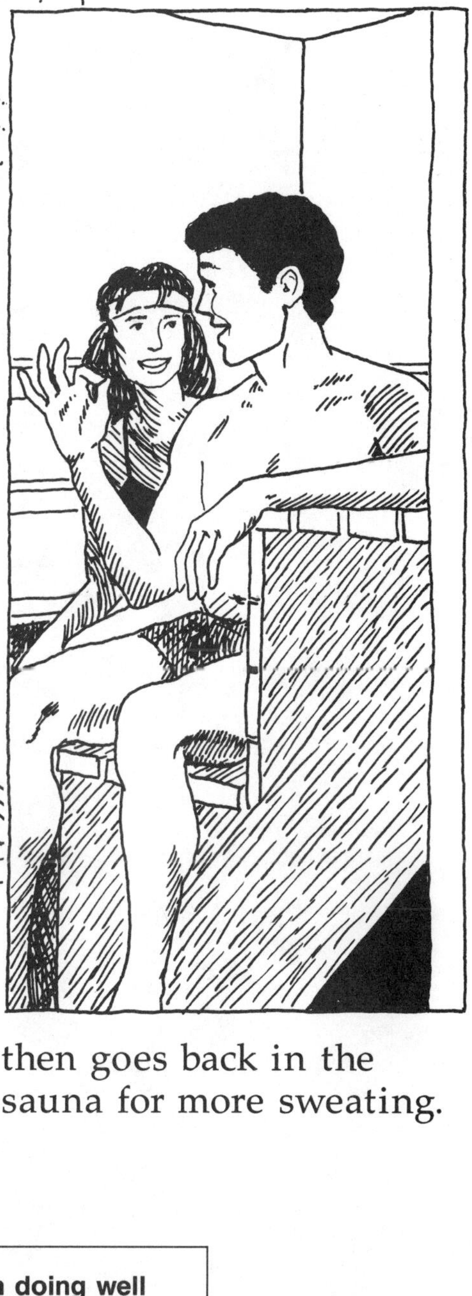

then goes back in the sauna for more sweating.

"I feel terrific physically and mentally. I am doing well at my job and in life since completing the Purification program. My senses have improved—I have better sight, smell and taste. And I don't get irritated with some people as I did before. The Purification program was a most worthwhile experience." —L.L.

There are no diets, no food fads. One just follows one's normal eating habits and is sure to eat plenty of vegetables which are not overcooked.

"Without a drug history, I had expected to get little from the Purification program. Instead I find myself with some valuable, positive and persisting gains. Clarity of thought and perception are improved. I now find myself with an expanded depth of field and periphery of vision. I am very pleased and surprised." —G.E.

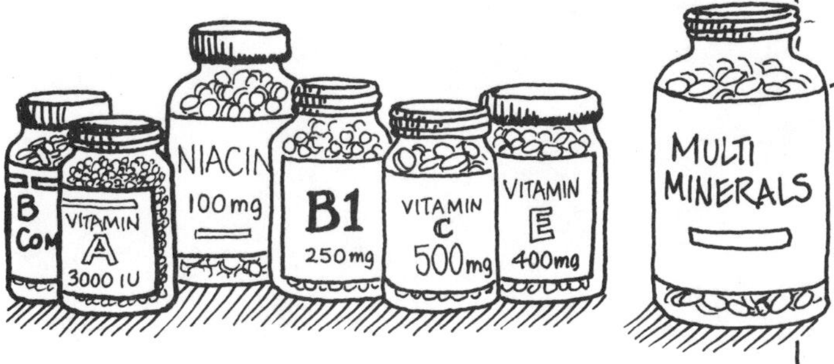

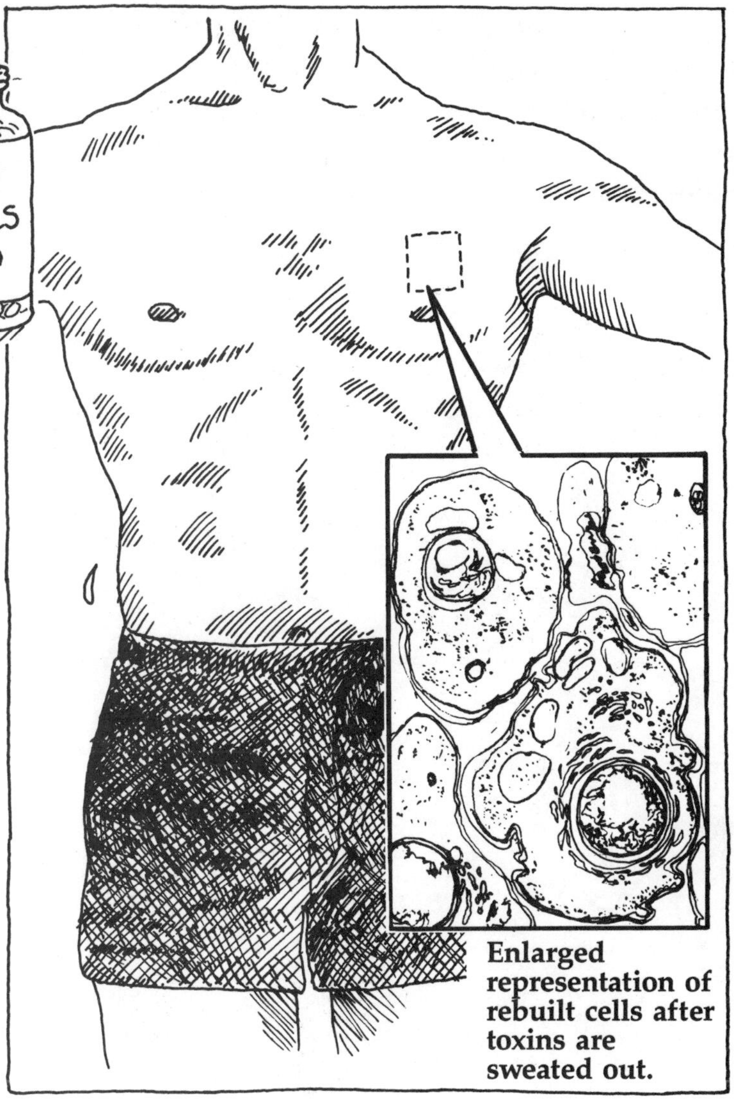

Enlarged representation of rebuilt cells after toxins are sweated out.

Nutrition in the form of certain vitamins and minerals is also an important part of the program. As drug deposits are flushed and sweated out of the body, extra vitamins and extra minerals are required:

- to repair the damage done by drugs,
- to rebuild the tissues and cells
- and to restore the body's biochemical balance.

These vitamins and minerals must be taken in the exact amounts advised.

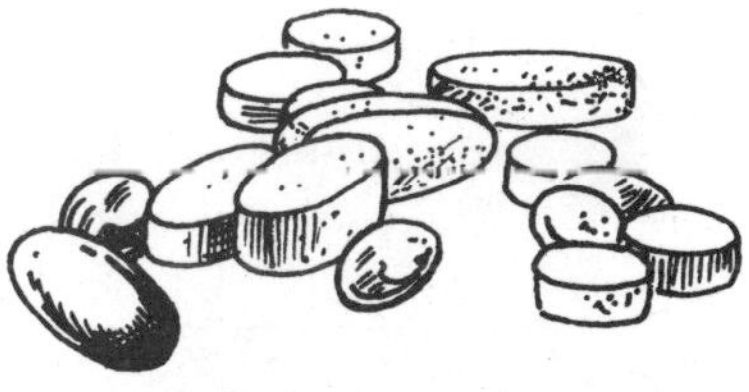

"The first week on the program I was very drowsy in the sauna. I realized this was from the anesthetic I had received during several operations. Later on the program this feeling disappeared and has not returned. I am feeling really great." —W.M.

Niacin, one of the B complex vitamins, is a *key* element in the way the program works. Its biochemical reaction is another of my early research discoveries.

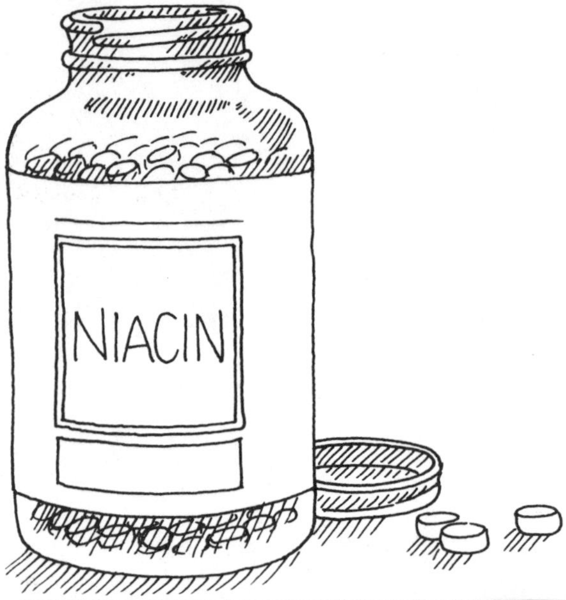

Niacin can produce some dramatic effects—it can turn on a very hot flush

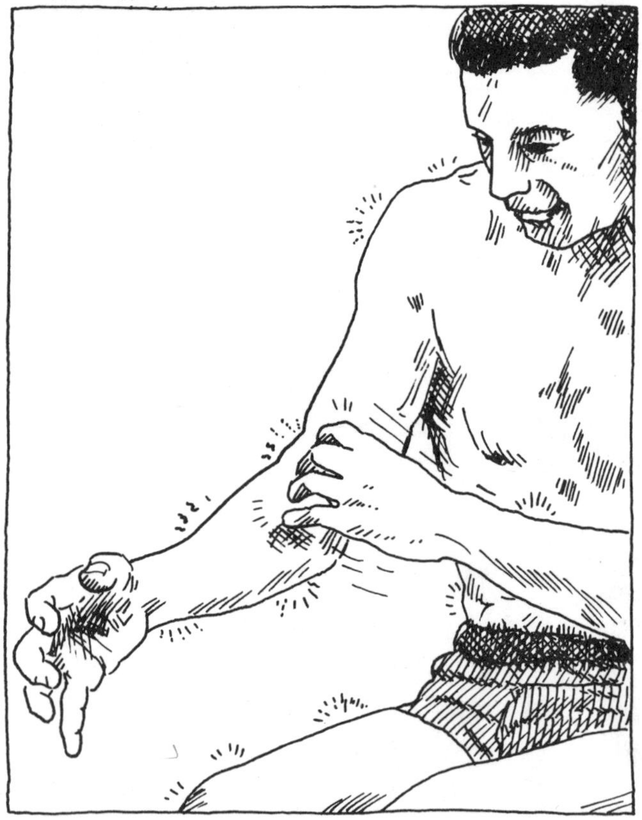

or prickly, itchy skin which can last for an hour or so.

"In the sauna a flush turned on with heavy itching. I felt spaced out, same as when I took mescaline. Then felt dull and stupid for about an hour and a half. This all blew off, leaving me feeling a lot brighter!" —A.D.

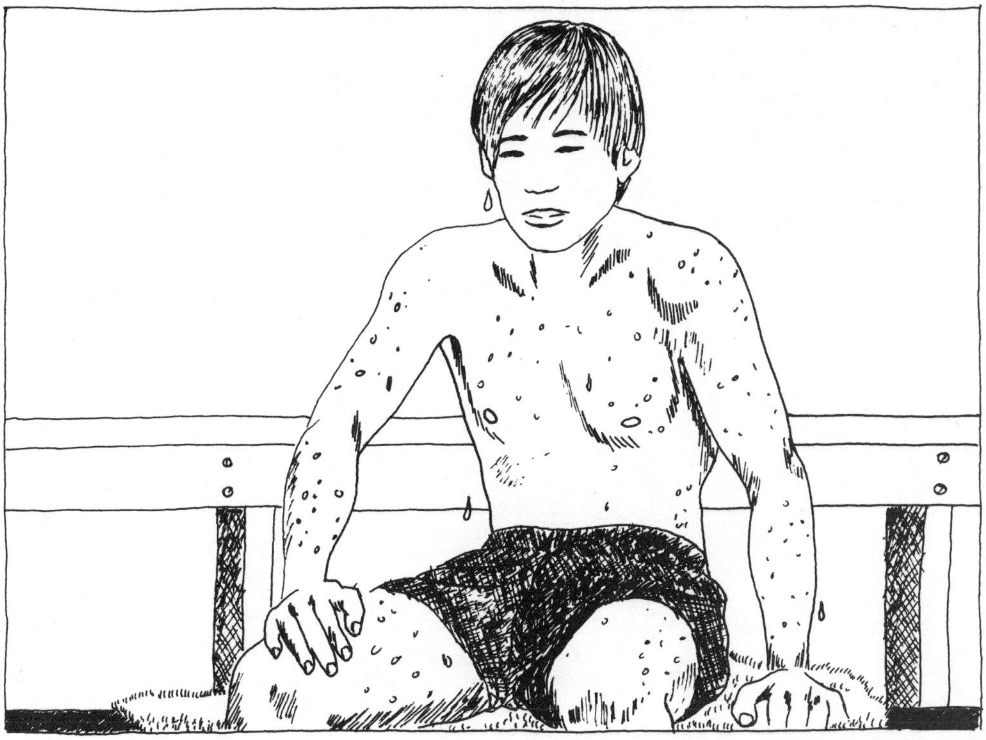

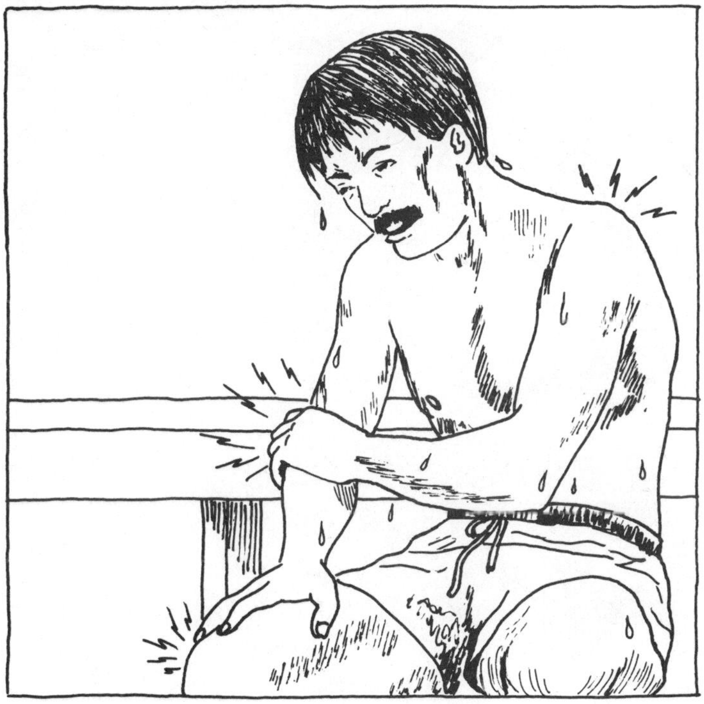

Niacin sometimes brings about other reactions, such as hives or aching bones or other effects, which may be uncomfortable temporarily.

Evidently these effects are simply the results of niacin interacting with niacin deficiencies which already exist in the cellular structure. Apparently niacin will do this as long as the program is continued standardly.

On the program niacin is taken in the *exact* amounts advised. This is very important for a successful result.

When enough niacin is taken in the right amounts, it appears to break up and unleash the drug and chemical deposits—including LSD crystals—from the body tissues and cells.

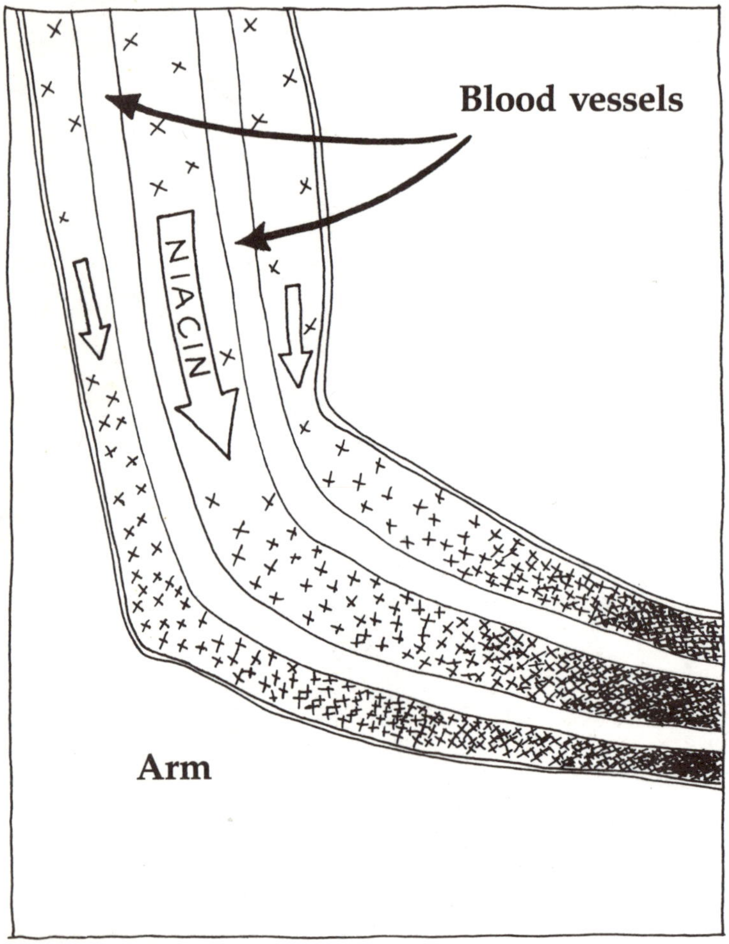

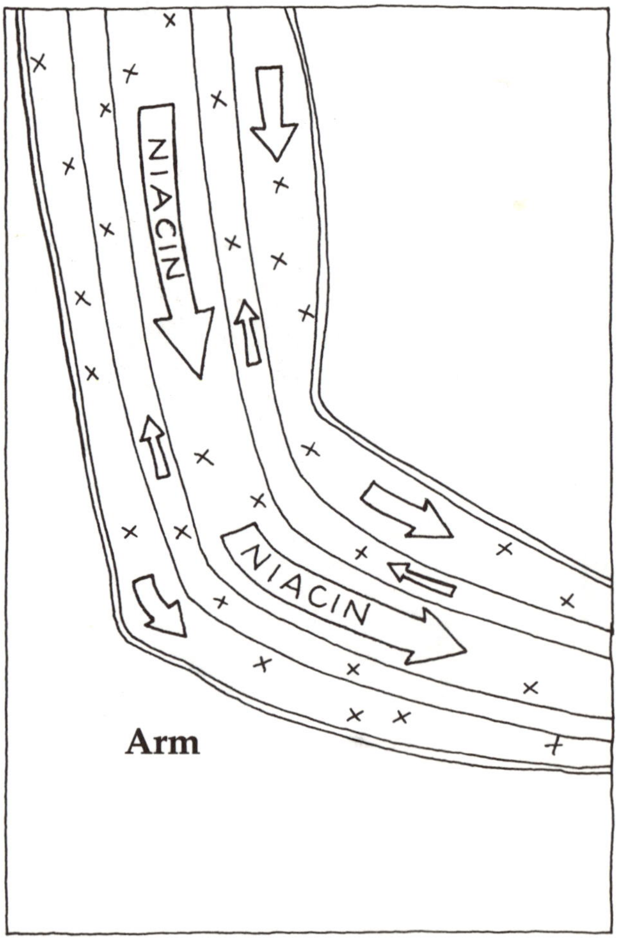

"The first day on the Purification program, after taking 100 mg. of niacin, I thought nothing had happened when suddenly I realized I was in the middle of an acid trip. I was stoned, very disoriented. This lasted half an hour, then dissipated. Since completing the program none of the 'trips' or sensations have recurred." —F.A.

Running and sweating must then be done daily to help flush these toxins out of the body.

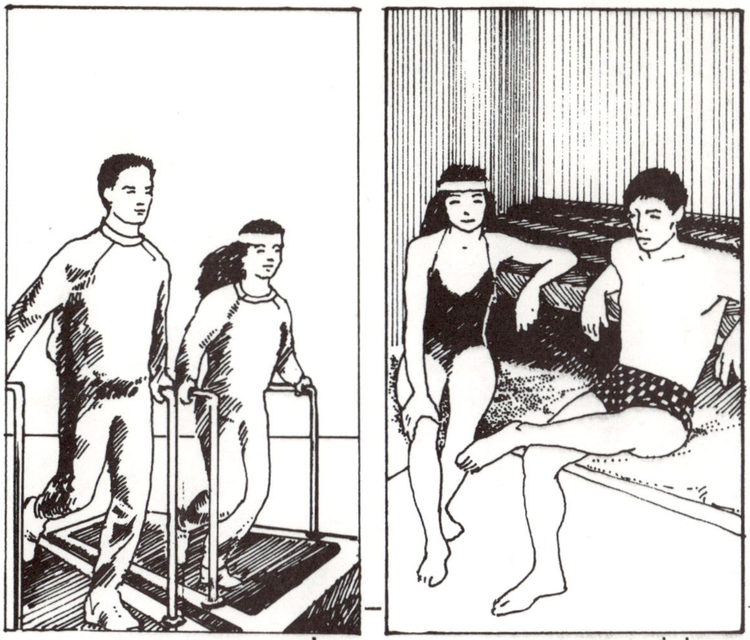

As drug residues tend to "lock up" mainly in the fatty tissues,

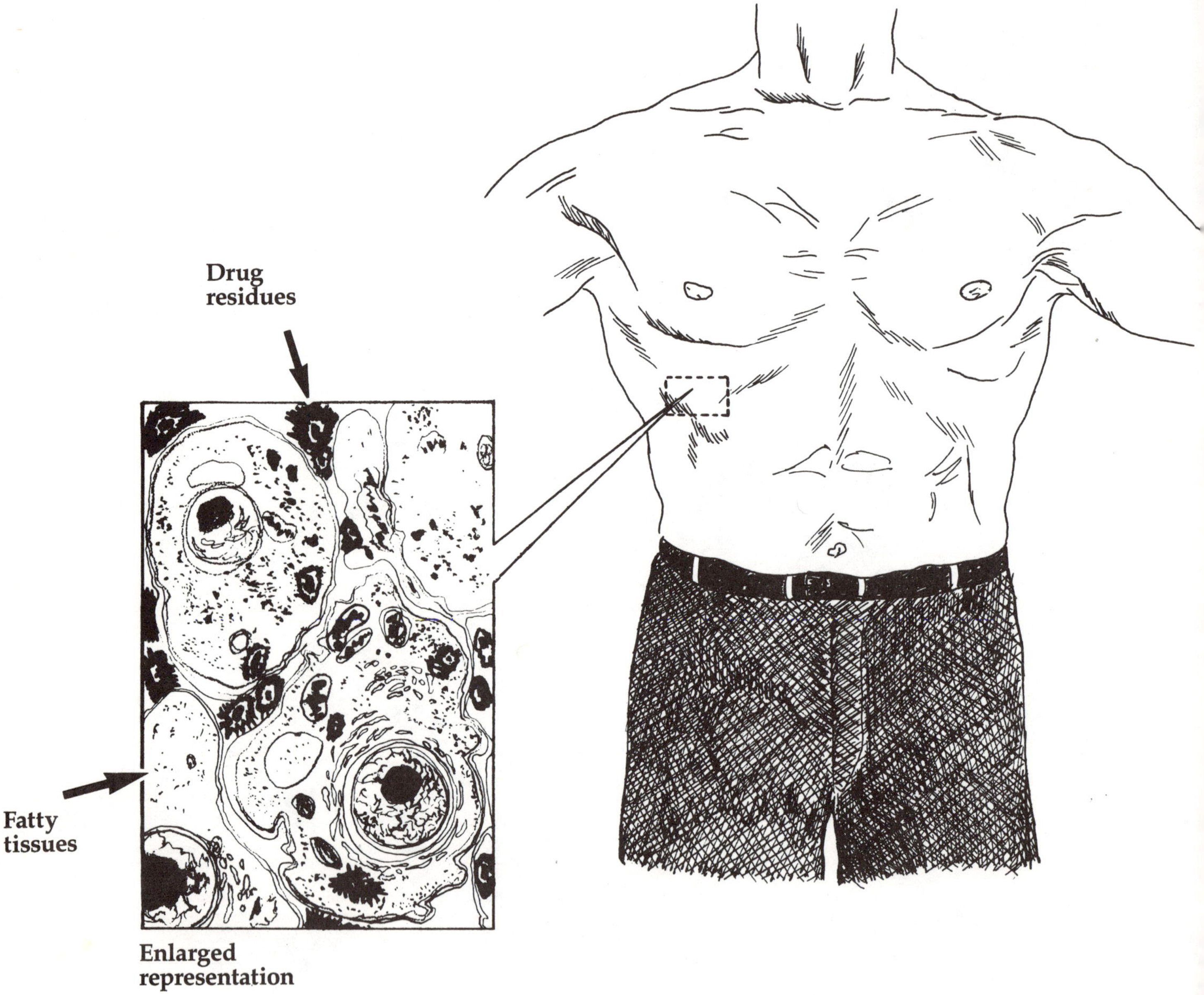

some oil is taken every day to encourage the body to give up its bad, drug-laden fat in exchange for the good oil.

The type of oil used on the Purification program is a mixture of four oils—soy, walnut, peanut and safflower oil—plus lecithin (a substance which appears to be capable of breaking fat into tiny particles which can pass readily into the tissues).

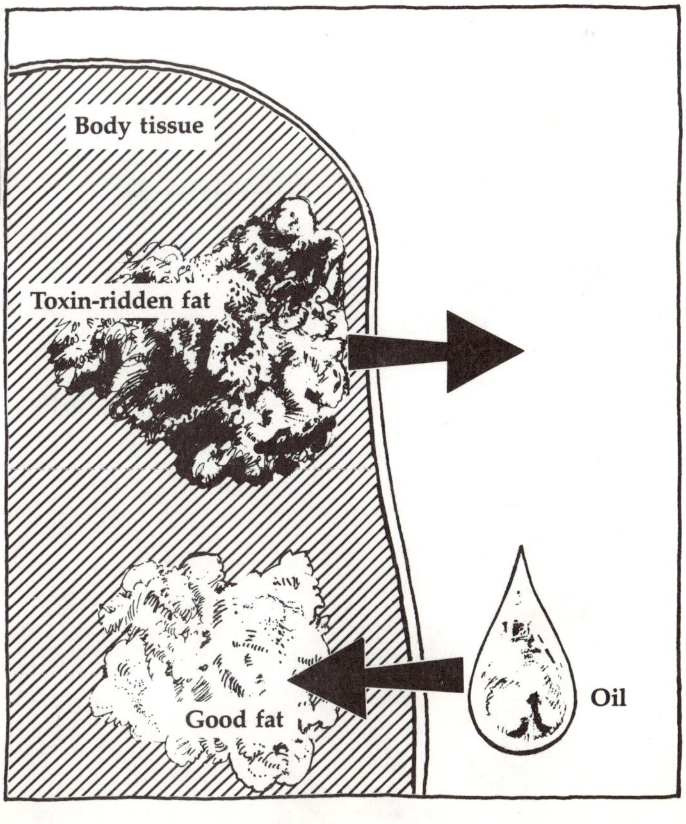

Calcium and magnesium are both important to the nervous system. Calcium is also vital in any healing or exchange process, as it is a basic building block.

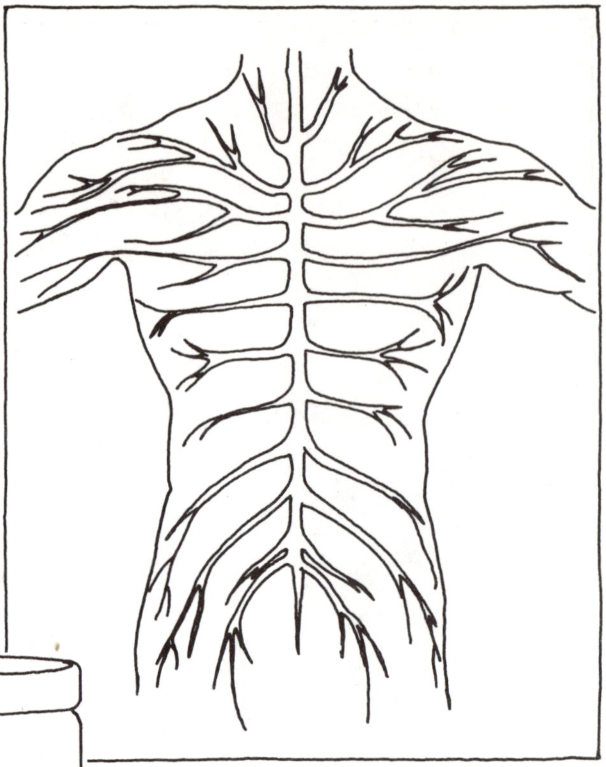

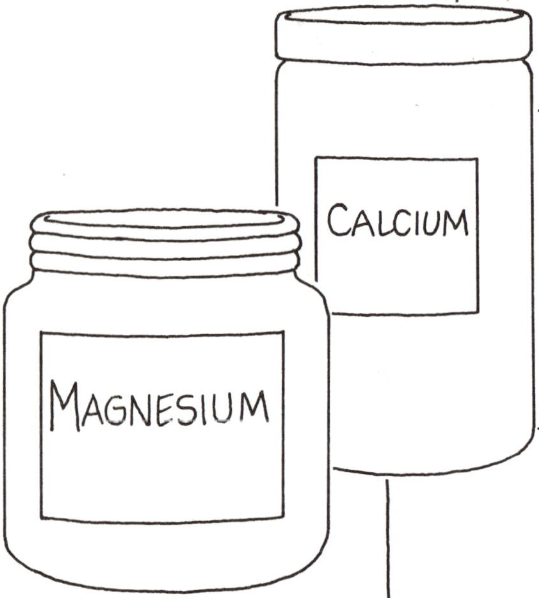

These are mixed in exact amounts in a special drink I developed in 1973, called "Cal-Mag."

Cal-Mag is taken daily on the Purification program

- to balance out the other minerals and vitamins,
- to handle and prevent deficiencies,
- to help rebuild cellular structure,
- to keep the nerves smoothed out,
- to help prevent sore muscles.

One follows *exactly* the instructions given for taking the vitamins, minerals, Cal-Mag and oil. They are *key* to completing the program successfully.

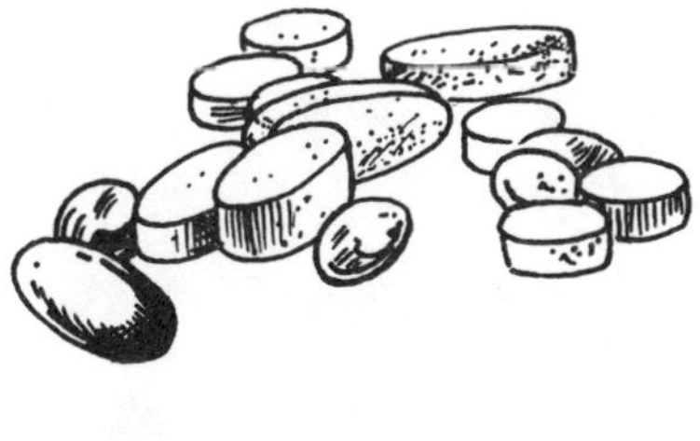

Tens of thousands of people the world over have now completed the Purification program.

According to research results and reports of people who have done the program, the effects of many drugs taken in the past and the effects of past medicines, anesthetics, sedatives or alcohol have "turned on,"

run through,

and then disappeared as their residues were sweated out on the Purification program.

"I went through several days of 'fog' and 'tilting and spinning' that reminded me of the sodium pentothal I'd received for operations, and a wild, tittery feeling from drugs and alcohol. The Purification program was the answer to the 'fog' and 'elsewhereness' that would sometimes kick in on me in life!" —E.A.

Another remarkable factor is—
because quantities of niacin are
taken

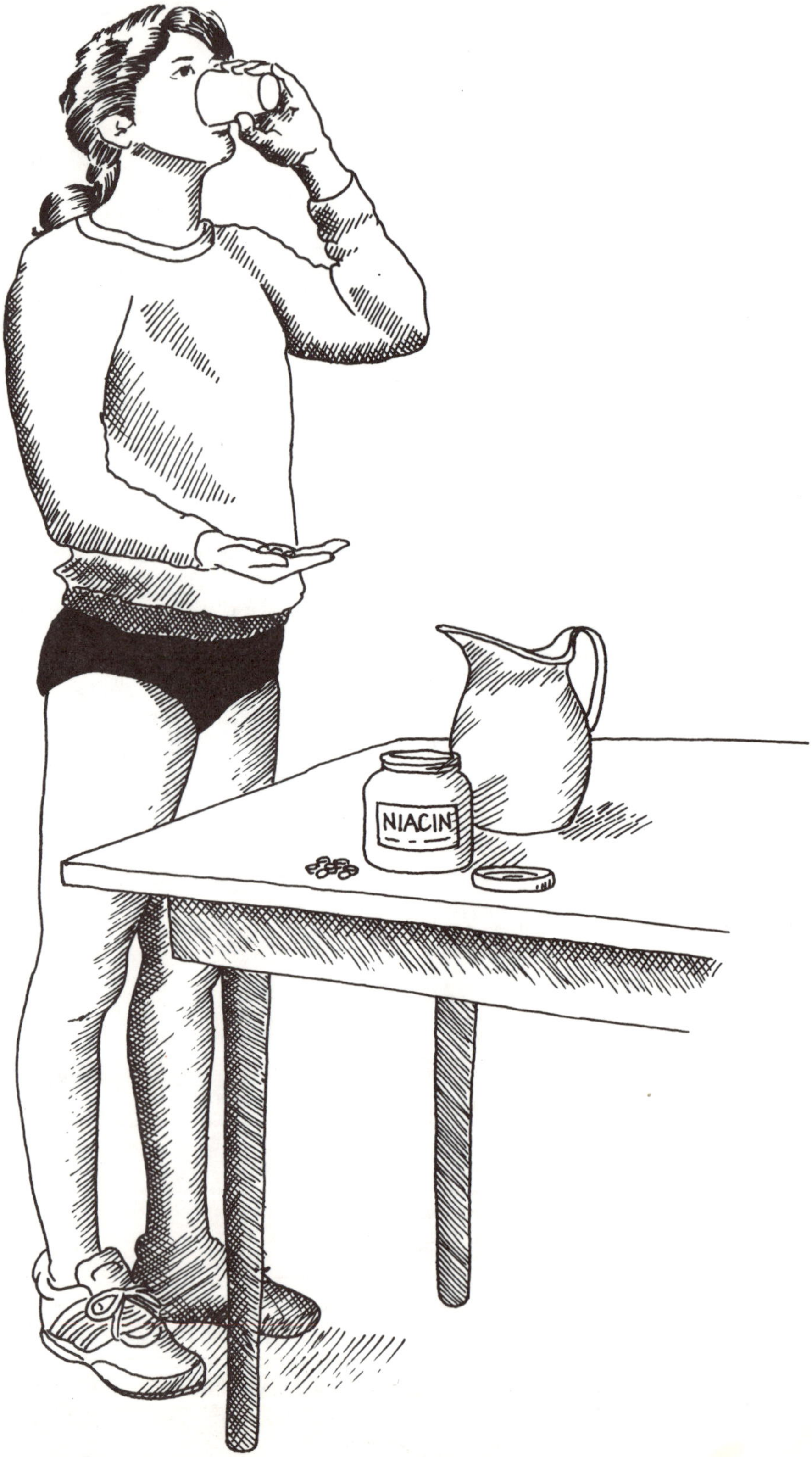

and because of the heat of the sauna—the program can have the effect of handling radiation.

"While doing this action all the symptoms of 'radiation sickness' turned on—vomiting, redness and prickliness of the skin. When the program was kept up, all of this disappeared and has not manifested itself again. I now feel much more alert." —W.M.

Some persons report that while doing the program

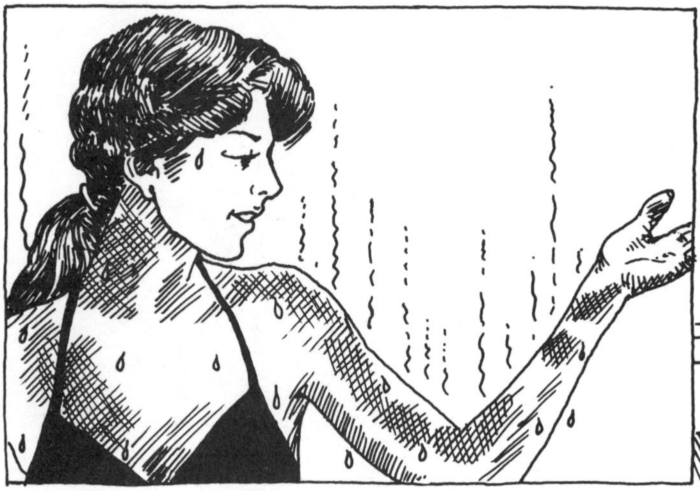

past sunburns "reappeared,"

lessened

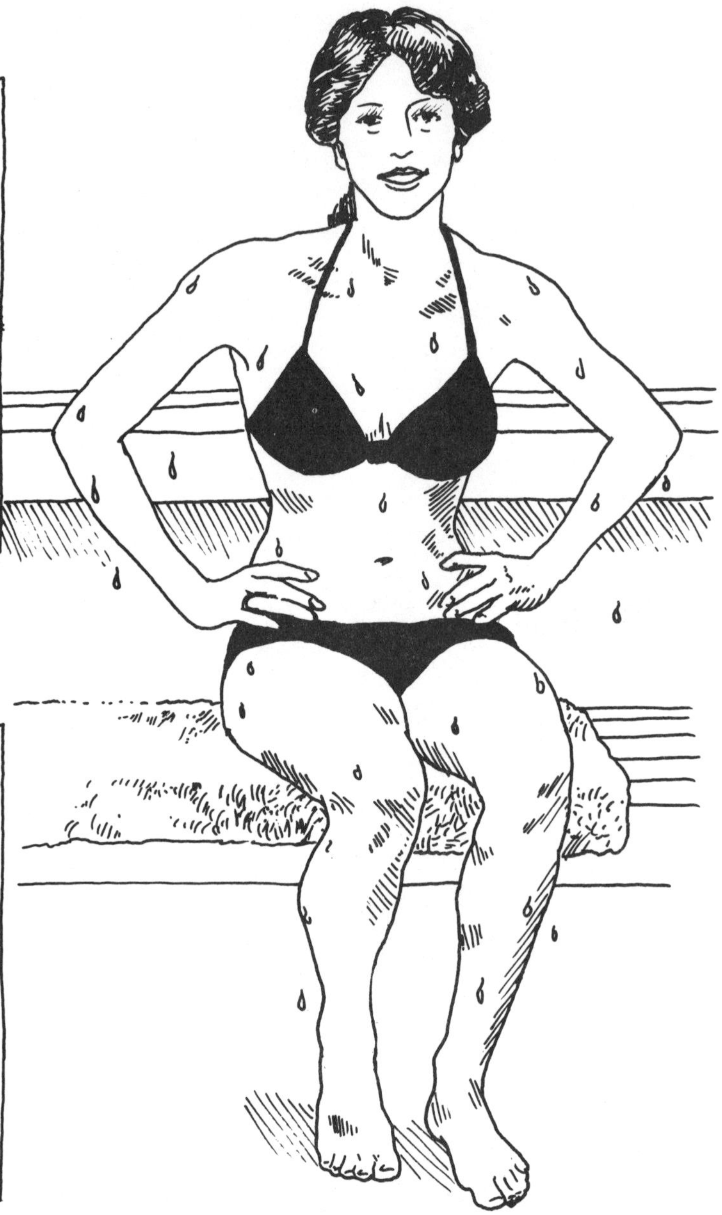

and left completely.

"On the program, I turned on a flush—like a sunburn—with a bathing suit outline. All of this then blew, I woke up this morning much more alert and brighter than usual." —S.M.

Or symptoms identified with past X-ray exposure

have "turned on,"

then diminished

and disappeared.

"I have had many X-rays this life and other radiation. The reactions are gradually subsiding on the Purification program. They are almost gone." —T.E.

Some have reported that the effects of radiation fallout "turned on,"

"ran through"

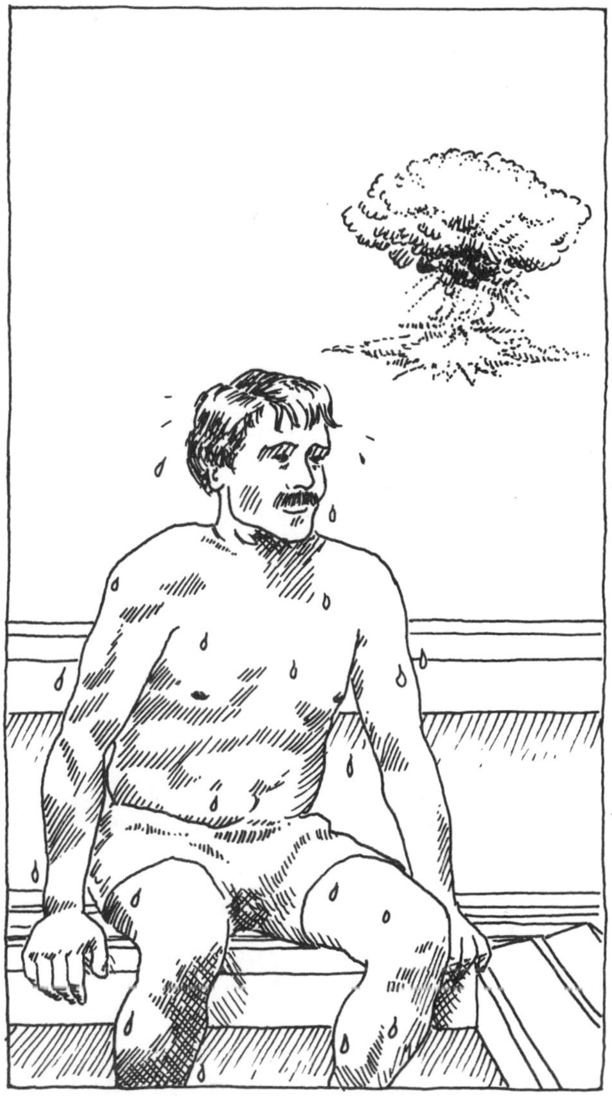

and then vanished while on the program.

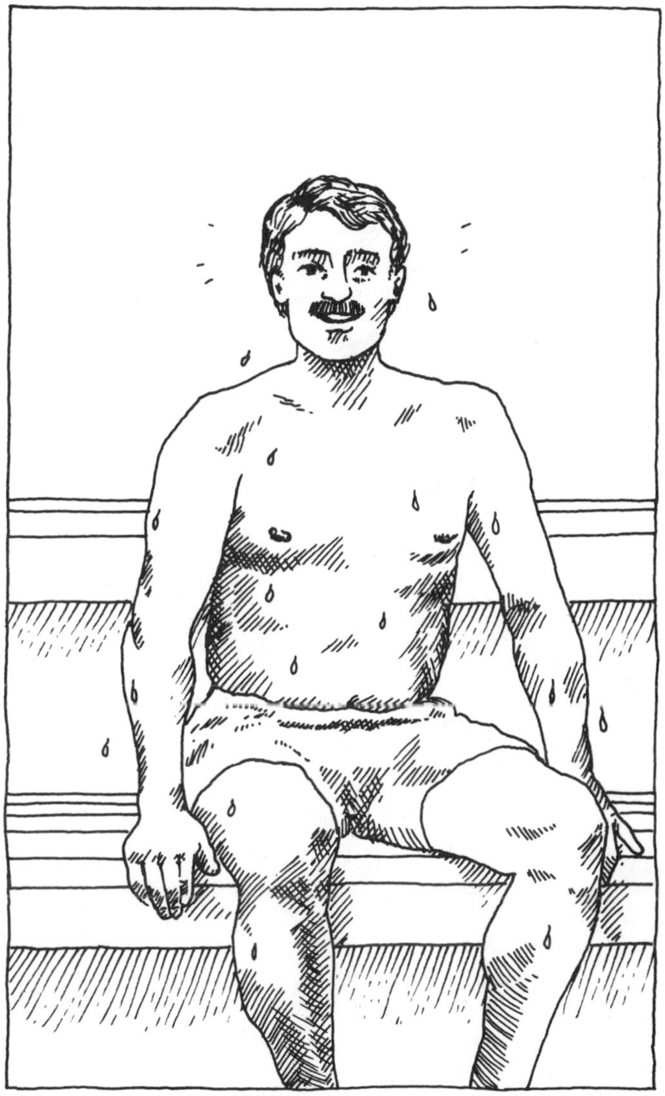

"I got a good deal of radiation from atomic blasts in 1953. I almost died from radiation burns at that time and from radiation fallout in the drinking water.

"At a point on the Purification program I felt the full return of that time with tremendous heat, swelling of the face and blisters and pain through to the bones. I felt the hate and anger of that moment, too. Some of my friends in Utah are dead from the atomic bomb tests. But I am alive and on the Purification program I went through these symptoms and they then vanished. It was a tremendous experience!" —H.J.

It may even be possible that the effects of Agent Orange (a highly toxic chemical which was used in the Vietnam War to strip living plants of their leaves) can be relieved on the Purification program. Some war veterans exposed to Agent Orange have reported "reexperiencing" its effects during sauna periods on the program.

Again, these effects restimulated, "ran through" and then ceased altogether, giving much relief.

"In the Vietnam War I was exposed to deadly poisonous gases and toxins, especially 'Agent Orange' and some sort of nerve gas. They inhibited my perceptions and control of my body and kept me from thinking straight and logically. From then on I considered my environment dangerous. On the Purification program I was brought out of that. These toxins and gases were fully flushed out. I feel healthy and in control of my body. Now life is definitely worthwhile to experience and create. I can say there is hope for Vietnam Vets." —W.B.

Whatever turns up in the program,
the routine is followed standardly,
day after day:

nutrition,

vitamins
and minerals,

oil,

Cal-Mag,

running,

sweating in the sauna,

plenty of sleep.

"I had had a skin fungus for about eighteen years that went away when I did the Purification program. All of my main senses—sight, taste, smell, etc.—seemed to improve as well." —P.G.

People experience many changes as the drug residuals are sweated out and their effects become less and less each day . . .

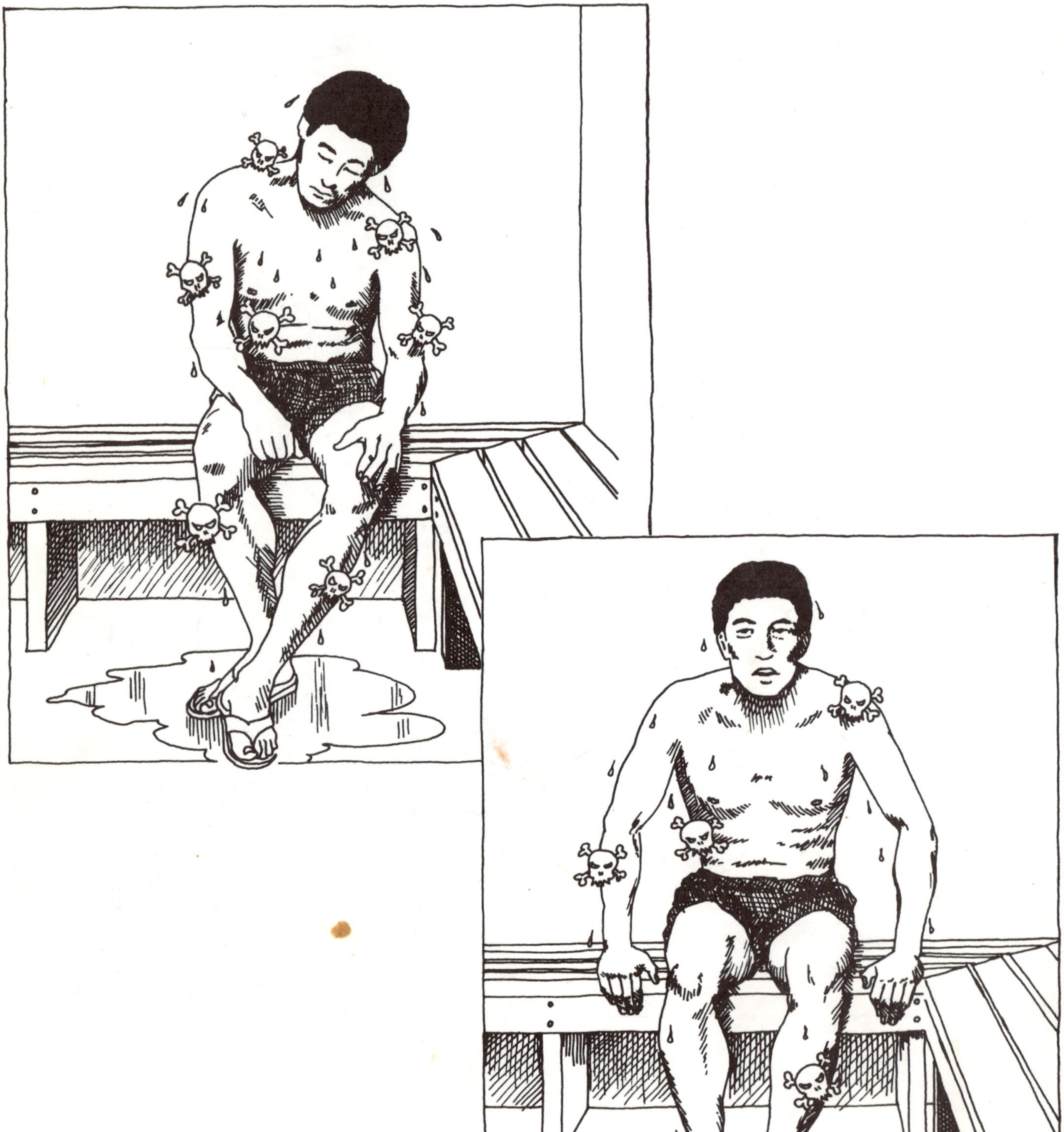

. . . until one no longer feels the effects of past drugs going into restimulation.

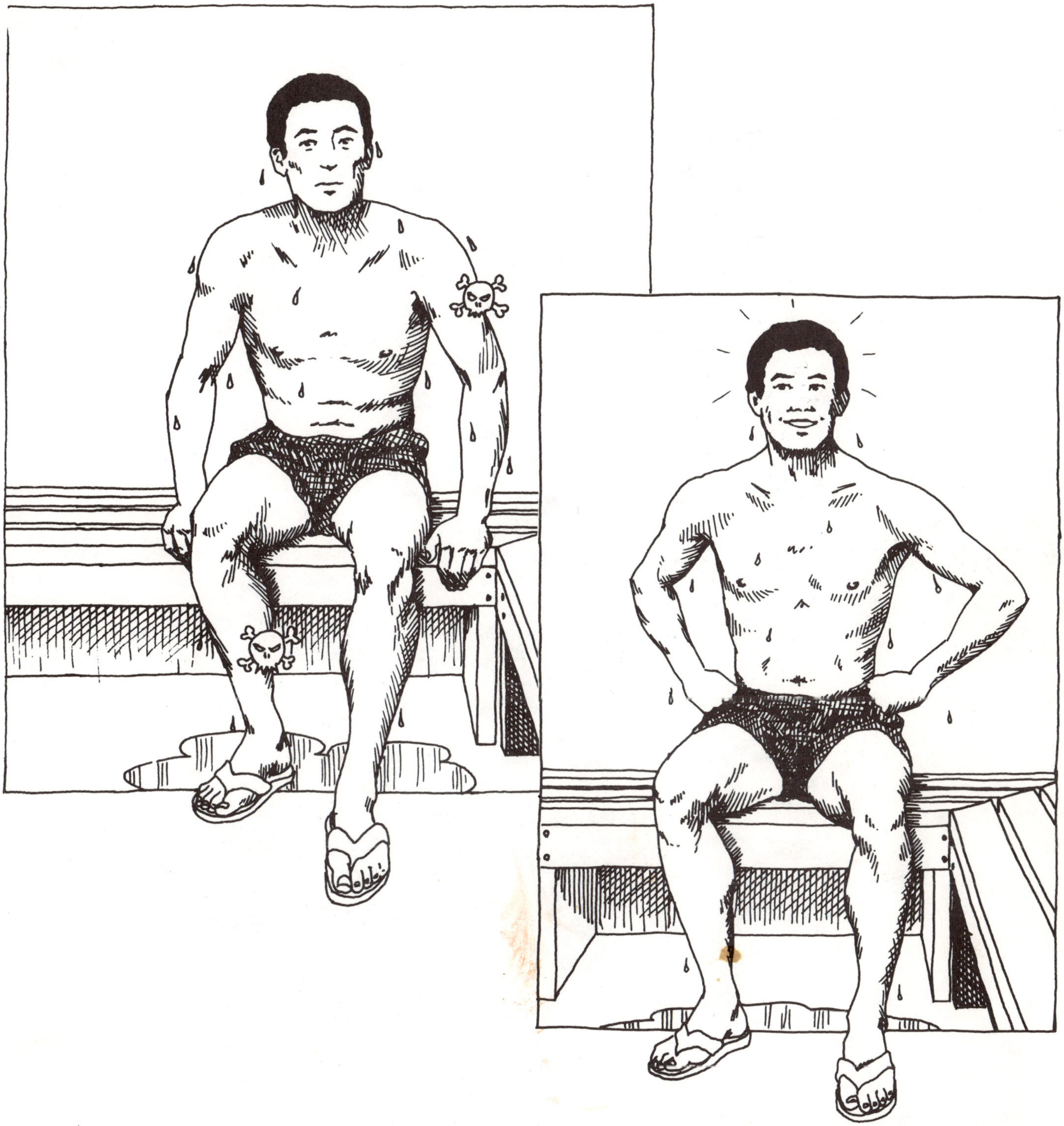

"This has been a truly fantastic program! I had many and various maladies, pains, aches and symptoms turn on and then disappear. But the most spectacular gains were not physical. My memory has improved. I feel brighter, more enthusiastic about life." —B.K.

Properly administered, this program is beyond price.

On the Purification program one is offering a person his life.

"After doing the Purification program I am alive! I once again feel like living and doing things I want to do. It's a great, new, fascinating feeling with unlimited dimensions!" —R.C.K.

Free of drug and toxic residuals and their restimulative effects, a person can make real mental and spiritual gains.

There is NO other program reported or known to handle the drug and toxic deposits that can be stored in the body.

The Purification program can be *the* answer to a drug-free society and a drug-free planet!

ENROLL ON THE PURIFICATION PROGRAM TODAY!

(A list of Scientology organizations that deliver the Purification program is on pages 99 through 103.)

Where to Do the Purification Program

For information on where to do the Purification program, contact the nearest Scientology church or organization listed at the back of this book or call this toll-free number:

Call: 1-800-334-LIFE in the US and Canada

Churches of Scientology have been delivering the Purification program as part of its spiritual counseling procedures since its release in 1979.

You can call this toll-free number 7 days a week from 9 A.M. to 11 P.M. Pacific Standard Time.

“I am always happy to hear from my readers.”

L. Ron Hubbard

These were the words of L. Ron Hubbard, who was always very interested in hearing from his friends and readers. He made a point of staying in communication with everyone he came in contact with over his fifty-year career as a professional writer, and he had thousands of fans and friends that he corresponded with all over the world.

The publishers of L. Ron Hubbard's works wish to continue this tradition and welcome letters and comments from you, his readers, both old and new.

Additionally, the publishers will be happy to send you information on anything you would like to know about Ron, his extraordinary life and accomplishments and the vast number of books he has written.

Any message addressed to the Author's Affairs Director at Bridge Publications will be given prompt and full attention.

Bridge Publications, Inc.
4751 Fountain Avenue
Los Angeles, California 90029
USA

Has your body become a toxic waste dump?

Everyone agrees we live today in an environment polluted by drugs, chemicals, toxins, pesticides, radiation. But L. Ron Hubbard's research, confirmed by clinical tests, found that these poisons accumulate in the fatty tissues of your body. They cloud your thinking and perceptions long after you have stopped using them.

Like a clear, flowing stream, the *Purification Rundown*® washes away these impurities — leaving you feeling sharper, more emotionally stable, and able to think more clearly.

Purification: An Illustrated Answer to Drugs has introduced you to the *Purification Rundown.* Now get the full data: the exact technology of this phenomenally successful program, how it was developed, and the results it produces.

Buy and read *Clear Body, Clear Mind: The Effective Purification Program*. This brand-new, comprehensive textbook by L. Ron Hubbard gives you the technology that can restore you to a clear body and a clear mind. Get your copy at a bookstore *today.*

If unavailable, order from Bridge Publications Mail Order, 4751 Fountain Ave., Los Angeles, CA 90029 USA, or NEW ERA Publications International ApS., Store Kongensgade 55, 1264 Copenhagen K, Denmark.

Get Your Free Catalog of Knowledge on How to Improve Life

L. Ron Hubbard's books and tapes increase your ability to understand yourself and others. His works give you the practical know-how you need to improve your life and the lives of your family and friends.

Many more materials by L. Ron Hubbard are available than have been covered in the pages of this book. A free catalog of these materials is available on request.

Write for your free catalog today!

Bridge Publications, Inc.
4751 Fountain Avenue
Los Angeles, California 90029

NEW ERA Publications International, ApS
Store Kongensgade 55
1264 Copenhagen K, Denmark

OTHER BOOKS AND TAPES BY L. RON HUBBARD

More books and cassettes by L. Ron Hubbard are available. Contact the Scientology organization nearest you (addresses pages 97 to 101) for any of these materials, or order directly from the publisher.

Basic Scientology Books

The Basic Scientology Books Package contains the knowledge you need to be able to improve conditions in life. These books are available individually or as a set, complete with an attractive slipcase.

Scientology: The Fundamentals of Thought
Improve life *and* make a better world with this easy-to-read book that lays out the fundamental truths about life and thought. No such knowledge has ever before existed, and no such results have ever before been attainable as those which can be reached by the use of this knowledge. Equipped with this book alone, one could perform seeming miracles in changing the states of health, ability and intelligence of people. This *is* how life works. This *is* how you change men, women and children for the better, and attain greater personal freedom.

A New Slant on Life
Have you ever asked yourself Who am I? What am I? This book of articles by L. Ron Hubbard answers these all-too-common questions. This is knowledge one can use every day—for a new, more confident and happier slant on life!

The Problems of Work
Work plays a big part in the game of life. Do you really enjoy your work? Are you certain of your job security? Would you like the increased personal satisfaction of doing your work well? This is the book that shows exactly how to achieve these things and more. The game of life—and within it, the game of work—can be enjoyable and rewarding.

Scientology 0-8: The Book of Basics
What is life? Did you know an individual can create space, energy and time? Here are the basics of life itself, and the secrets of becoming cause over any area of your life. Discover how you can use the data in this book to achieve your goals.

Basic Dictionary of Dianetics and Scientology

Compiled from the works of L. Ron Hubbard, this convenient dictionary contains the terms and expressions needed by anyone learning Dianetics and Scientology technology. And a *special bonus*—an easy-to-read Scientology organizing board chart that shows you who to contact for services and information at your nearest Scientology organization.

Basic Dianetics Books

The Basic Dianetics Books Package is your complete guide to the inner workings of the mind. You can get all of these books individually or in a set, complete with an attractive slipcase.

Dianetics: The Modern Science of Mental Health

Acclaimed as the most effective self-help book ever published. Dianetics technology has helped millions reach new heights of freedom and ability. Millions of copies are sold every year! Discover the source of mental barriers that prevent you from achieving your goals—and how to handle them!

The Dynamics of Life

Break through the barriers to your happiness. This is the first book Ron wrote detailing the startling principles behind Dianetics—facts so powerful they can change forever the way you look at yourself and your potentials. Discover how you can use the powerful basic principles in this book to blast through the barriers of your mind and gain full control over your success, future and happiness.

Self Analysis

The complete do-it-yourself handbook for anyone who wants to improve their abilities and success potential. Use the simple, easy-to-learn techniques in *Self Analysis* to build self-confidence and reduce stress.

Dianetics: The Evolution of a Science

It is estimated that we use less than ten percent of our mind's potential. What stops us from developing and using the full potential of our minds? *Dianetics: The Evolution of a Science* is L. Ron Hubbard's incredible story of how he discovered the reactive mind and how he developed the keys to unlock its secrets. Get this firsthand account of what the mind really is, and how you can release its hidden potential.

Dianetics Graduate Books

These books by L. Ron Hubbard give you detailed knowledge of how the mind works—data you can use to help yourself and others break out of the traps of life. While you can get these books individually, the Dianetics Graduate

Books Package can also be purchased as a set, complete with an attractive slipcase.

Science of Survival

If you ever wondered why people act the way they do, you'll find this book a wealth of information. It's vital to anyone who wants to understand others and improve personal relationships. *Science of Survival* is built around a remarkable chart—the Hubbard Chart of Human Evaluation. With it you can understand and predict other people's behavior and reactions and greatly increase your control over your own life. This is a valuable handbook that can make a difference between success and failure on the job and in life.

Dianetics 55!

Your success in life depends on your ability to communicate. Do you know a formula exists for communication? Learn the rules of better communication that can help you live a more fulfilling life. Here, L. Ron Hubbard deals with the fundamental principles of communication and how you can master these to achieve your goals.

Advanced Procedure and Axioms

For the *first* time the basics of thought and the physical universe have been codified into a set of fundamental laws, signaling an entirely new way to view and approach the subjects of man, the physical universe and even life itself.

Handbook for Preclears

Written as an advanced personal workbook, *Handbook for Preclears* contains easily done processes to help you overcome the effect of times you were not in control of your life, times that your emotions were a barrier to your success and much more. Completing all the fifteen auditing steps contained in this book sets you up for really being in *control* of your environment and life.

Child Dianetics

Here is a revolutionary new approach to rearing children with Dianetics auditing techniques. Find out how you can help your child achieve greater confidence, more self-reliance, improved learning rate and a happier, more loving relationship with you.

Notes on the Lectures of L. Ron Hubbard

Compiled from his fascinating lectures given shortly after the publication of *Dianetics,* this book contains some of the first material Ron ever released on the ARC triangle and the Tone Scale, and how these discoveries relate to auditing.

OT[1] Library Package

All the following books contain the knowledge of a spiritual being's relationship to this universe and how his abilities to operate successfully in it can be restored. You can get all of these books individually or in a set, complete with an attractive slipcase.

Scientology 8-80

What are the laws of life? We are all familiar with physical laws such as the law of gravity, but what laws govern life and thought? L. Ron Hubbard answers the riddles of life and its goals in the physical universe.

Scientology 8-8008

Get the basic truths about your nature as a spiritual being and your relationship to the physical universe around you. Here, L. Ron Hubbard describes procedures designed to increase your abilities to heights previously only dreamed of.

Scientology: A History of Man

A fascinating look at the evolutionary background and history of the human race—revolutionary concepts guaranteed to intrigue you and challenge many basic assumptions about man's true power, potential and abilities.

The Creation of Human Ability

This book contains processes designed to restore the power of a thetan over his own postulates, to understand the nature of his beingness, to free his self-determinism and much, much more.

Basic Executive Books

The Basic Executive Books Package consists of the book *The Problems of Work* and the two books listed below. They are available individually or as a set, complete with an attractive slipcase.

How to Live Though an Executive

What are the factors in business and commerce which, if lacking, can keep a person overworked and worried, keep labor and management at each

---

1. **OT:** abbreviation for **Operating Thetan,** a state of beingness. It is a being "at cause over matter, energy, space, time, form and life." *Operating* comes from "able to operate without dependency on things," and *thetan* is the Greek letter *theta* (θ), which the Greeks used to represent *thought* or perhaps *spirit,* to which an *n* is added to make a noun in the modern style used to create words in engineering. It is also θ^n or "theta to the nth degree," meaning unlimited or vast.

other's throats, and make an unsafe working atmosphere? L. Ron Hubbard reveals principles based on years of research into many different types of organizations.

Introduction to Scientology Ethics

A complete knowledge of ethics is vital to anyone's success in life. Without knowing and applying the information in this book, success is only a matter of luck or chance. That is not much to look forward to. This book contains the answers to questions like, "How do I know when a decision is right or wrong?" "How can I predictably improve things around me?" The powerful ethics technology of L. Ron Hubbard is your way to ever-increasing survival.

Other Scientology Books

Have You Lived Before This Life?

This is the book that sparked a flood of interest in the ancient puzzle: Does man live only one life? The answer lay in mystery, buried until L. Ron Hubbard's researches unearthed the truth. Actual case histories of people recalling past lives in auditing tell the tale.

Dianetics and Scientology Technical Dictionary

This dictionary is your indispensable guide to the words and ideas of Scientology and Dianetics technologies—technologies which can help you increase your know-how and effectiveness in life. Over three thousand words are defined—including a new understanding of vital words like *life, love* and *happiness* as well as Scientology terms.

Modern Management Technology Defined: Hubbard Dictionary of Administration and Management

Here's a real breakthrough in the subject of administration and management! Eighty-six hundred words are defined for greater understanding of any business situation. Clear, precise Scientology definitions describe many previously baffling phenomena and bring truth, sanity and understanding to the often murky field of business management.

Organization Executive Course

The *Organization Executive Course* volumes contain organizational technology never before known to man. This is not just how a Scientology organization works; this is how the operation of *any* organization, *any* activity, can be improved. A person knowing the data in these volumes fully, and applying it, could completely reverse any downtrend in a company—or even a country!

Management Series Volumes 1 and 2

These books contain technology that anyone who works with management in any way must know completely to be a true success. Contained in these books are such subjects as data evaluation, the technology of how to organize any area for maximum production and expansion, how to handle personnel, the actual technology of public relations and much more.

Background and Ceremonies of the Church of Scientology

Discover the beautiful and inspiring ceremonies of the Church of Scientology, and its fascinating religious and historical background. This book contains the illuminating Creed of the Church, church services, sermons and ceremonies, many as originally given in person by L. Ron Hubbard, Founder of Scientology.

What Is Scientology?

Scientology applied religious philosophy has attracted great interest and attention since its beginning. What is Scientology philosophy? What can it accomplish—and why are so many people from all walks of life proclaiming its effectiveness? Find the answers to these questions and many others in *What Is Scientology?*

Introductory and Demonstration Processes and Assists

How can you help someone increase his enthusiasm for living? How can you improve someone's self-confidence on the job? Here are basic Scientology processes you can use to help others deal with life and living.

Volunteer Minister's Handbook

This is a big, practical how-to-do-it book to give a person the basic knowledge on how to help self and others through the rough spots in life. It consists of twenty-one sections—each one covering important situations in life, such as drug and alcohol problems, study difficulties, broken marriages, accidents and illnesses, a failing business, difficult children, and much more. This is the basic tool you need to help someone out of troubles, and bring about a happier life.

Classification, Gradation and Awareness Chart

Your route to higher levels of ability and self-confidence is fully mapped on the *Classification, Gradation and Awareness Chart*—also called The Bridge to Total Freedom. With this chart, you can find out where you are now and the exact sequence of Dianetics and Scientology services you will take as you move across The Bridge to higher states of existence.

The Personal Achievement Series

There are nearly three thousand recorded lectures by L. Ron Hubbard on the subjects of Dianetics and Scientology. What follows is a sampling of these lectures, each known and loved the world over. All of these are presented in Clearsound state-of-the-art sound-recording technology, notable for its clarity and brilliance of reproduction.

Get all the Personal Achievement Series cassettes by L. Ron Hubbard listed below and ask your nearest Scientology church or organization or the publisher about future releases.

The Story of Dianetics and Scientology

In this lecture, L. Ron Hubbard shares with you his earliest insights into human nature and gives a compelling and often humorous account of his experiences. Spend an unforgettable time with Ron as he talks about the start of Dianetics and Scientology!

The Road to Truth

The road to truth has eluded man since the beginning of time. In this classic lecture, L. Ron Hubbard explains what this road actually is and why it is the only road one MUST travel all the way once begun. This lecture reveals the only road to higher levels of living.

Scientology and Effective Knowledge

Voyage to new horizons of awareness! *Scientology and Effective Knowledge* by L. Ron Hubbard can help you understand more about yourself and others. A fascinating tale of the beginnings of Dianetics and Scientology.

The Deterioration of Liberty

What do governments fear so much in a population that they amass weapons to defend themselves from people? Find out from Ron in this classic lecture.

Power of Choice and Self-Determinism

Man's ability to determine the course of his life depends on his ability to exercise his power of choice. Find how you can increase your power of choice and self-determinism in life from Ron in this lecture.

Scientology and Ability

Ron points out that this universe is here because we perceive it and agree to it. Applying Scientology principles to life can bring new adventure to life and put you on the road to discovering better beingness.

The Hope of Man

Various men in history brought forth the idea that there was hope of improvement. But L. Ron Hubbard's discoveries in Dianetics and Scientology have made that hope a reality. Find out by listening to this lecture how Scientology has become man's one, true hope for his final freedom.

The Dynamics

In this lecture Ron gives incredible data on the dynamics: how man creates on them, what happens when a person gets stuck in just one; how wars relate to the third dynamic and much more.

Money

Ron talks in this classic lecture about that subject which makes or breaks men with the greatest of ease—money. Find out what money really is and gain greater control over your own finances.

Formulas for Success—*The Five Conditions*

How does one achieve real success? It sometimes appears that luck is the primary factor, but the truth of the matter is that natural laws exist which govern the conditions of life. These laws have been discovered by Ron, and in this lecture he gives you the exact steps to take in order to improve conditions in any aspect of your life.

Health and Certainty

You need certainty of yourself in order to achieve the success you want in life. In *Health and Certainty,* L. Ron Hubbard tells how you can achieve certainty and really be free to think for yourself. Get this tape now and start achieving your full potential!

Operation Manual for the Mind

Everybody has a mind—but who has an operation manual for it? This lecture reveals why man went on for thousands of years without understanding how his mind is supposed to work. The problem has been solved. Find out how with this tape.

Miracles

Why is it that man often loses to those forces he resists or opposes? Why can't an individual simply overcome obstacles in life and win? In the tape lecture *Miracles,* L. Ron Hubbard describes why one suffers losses in life. He also describes how a person can experience the miracles of happiness, self-fulfillment and winning at life. Get a copy today.

The Road to Perfection—*The Goodness of Man*

Unlike earlier practices that sought to "improve" man because he was "bad," Scientology assumes that you have *good* qualities that simply need to be *increased.* In *The Road to Perfection,* L. Ron Hubbard shows how workable this assumption really is—and how you can begin to use your mind, talents and abilities to the fullest. Get this lecture and increase your ability to handle life.

The Dynamic Principles of Existence

What does it take to survive in today's world? It's not something you learn much about in school. You have probably gotten a lot of advice about how to "get along." *Your survival right now is limited by the data you were given.* This lecture describes the dynamic principles of existence, and tells how you can use these principles to increase your success in all areas of life. Happiness and self-esteem *can* be yours. Don't settle for anything less.

Man: Good or Evil?

In this lecture, L. Ron Hubbard explores the greatest mystery that has confronted modern science and philosophy—the true nature of man's livingness and beingness. Is man simply a sort of wind-up doll or clock—or worse, an evil beast with no control of his cravings? Or is he capable of reaching higher levels of ability, awareness and happiness? Get this tape and find out the *real* answers.

Differences between Scientology and Other Studies

The most important questions in life are the ones you started asking as a child: What happens to a person when he dies? Is man basically good, or is he evil? What are the intentions of the world toward me? Did my mother and father really love me? What is love? Unlike other studies, which try to *force* you to think a certain way, Scientology enables you to find your own answers. Listen to this important lecture. It will put you on the road to true understanding and belief in yourself.

The Machinery of the Mind

We do a lot of things "automatically"—such as driving a car. But what happens when a person's mental machinery takes over and starts running him? In this fascinating lecture, L. Ron Hubbard gives you an understanding of what mental machinery really is, and how it can cause a person to lose control. You *can* regain your power of decision and be in full control of your life. Listen to this lecture and find out how.

The Affinity–Reality–Communication Triangle

Have you ever tried to talk to an angry man? Have you ever tried to get something across to someone who is really in fear? Have you ever known someone who was impossible to cheer up? Listen to this fascinating lecture by L. Ron Hubbard and learn how you can use the affinity-reality-communication triangle to resolve personal relationships. By using the data in this lecture, you can better understand others and live a happier life.

Increasing Efficiency

Inefficiency is a major barrier to success. How can you increase your efficiency? Is it a matter of changing your diet, or adjusting your working environment? These approaches have uniformly failed, because they overlook the most important element: *you.* L. Ron Hubbard has found those factors that *can* increase your efficiency, and he reveals it in this timely lecture. Get *Increasing Efficiency* now, and start achieving *your* full potential.

Man's Relentless Search

For countless centuries, man has been trying to find himself. Why does this quest repeatedly end in frustration and disappointment? What is he *really* looking for, and why can't he find it? For the real truth about man and life, listen to this taped lecture by L. Ron Hubbard, *Man's Relentless Search.* Restore your belief in yourself!

More advanced books and lectures are available. Contact your nearest organization or write directly to the publisher for a full catalog.

CHURCH AND ORGANIZATION ADDRESS LIST

United States of America

Albuquerque

Church of Scientology
8106 Menaul Blvd. NE
Albuquerque, New Mexico 87110

Ann Arbor

Church of Scientology
301 North Ingalls Street
Ann Arbor, Michigan 48104

Atlanta

Church of Scientology
2632 Piedmonte Rd., NE
Atlanta, Georgia 30324

Austin

Church of Scientology
2200 Guadalupe
Austin, Texas 78705

Boston

Church of Scientology
448 Beacon Street
Boston, Massachusetts 02115

Buffalo

Church of Scientology
47 West Huron Street
Buffalo, New York 14202

Chicago

Church of Scientology
3011 North Lincoln Avenue
Chicago, Illinois 60657

Cincinnati

Church of Scientology
215 West 4th Street, 5th Floor
Cincinnati, Ohio 45202

Clearwater

Church of Scientology
Flag® Service Organization
210 South Fort Harrison Avenue
Clearwater, Florida 34616

Columbus

Church of Scientology
167 East State Street
Columbus, Ohio 43215

Dallas

Church of Scientology
Celebrity Centre® Dallas
8501 Manderville Lane
Dallas, Texas 75231

Denver

Church of Scientology
375 South Navajo Street
Denver, Colorado 80223

Detroit

Church of Scientology
321 Williams Street
Royal Oak, Michigan 48067

Honolulu

Church of Scientology
1 N. King St., Lower Level
Honolulu, Hawaii 96817

Kansas City

Church of Scientology
3619 Broadway
Kansas City, Missouri 64111

Las Vegas

Church of Scientology
846 East Sahara Avenue
Las Vegas, Nevada 89104

Church of Scientology
Celebrity Centre Las Vegas
1100 South 10th Street
Las Vegas, Nevada 89104-1505

Long Island

Church of Scientology
330 Fulton Avenue
Hempstead, New York 11550

Los Angeles and vicinity

Church of Scientology
4810 Sunset Boulevard
Los Angeles, California 90027

Church of Scientology
1451 Irvine Boulevard
Tustin, California 92680

Church of Scientology
99 East Colorado Boulevard
Pasadena, California 91150

Church of Scientology
10335 Magnolia Boulevard
North Hollywood, California 91601

Church of Scientology
American Saint Hill Organization
1413 North Berendo Street
Los Angeles, California 90027

Church of Scientology
American Saint Hill Foundation
1413 North Berendo Street
Los Angeles, California 90027

Church of Scientology
Advanced Organization of
Los Angeles
1306 North Berendo Street
Los Angeles, California 90027

Church of Scientology
Celebrity Centre International
5930 Franklin Avenue
Hollywood, California 90028

Miami

Church of Scientology
120 Giralda Avenue
Coral Gables, Florida 33134

Minneapolis

Church of Scientology
3019 Minnehaha Avenue
Minneapolis, Minnesota 55406

New Haven

Church of Scientology
909 Whalley Avenue
New Haven, Connecticut 06515

New York City

Church of Scientology
227 West 46th Street
New York City, New York 10036

Church of Scientology
Celebrity Centre New York
65 East 82nd Street
New York City, New York 10028

Orlando

Church of Scientology
710-A East Colonial Drive
Orlando, Florida 32803

Philadelphia

Church of Scientology
1315 Race Street
Philadelphia, Pennsylvania 19107

Phoenix

Church of Scientology
4450 North Central Avenue, Suite 102
Phoenix, Arizona 85012

Portland

Church of Scientology
323 SW Washington
Portland, Oregon 97204

Church of Scientology
Celebrity Centre Portland
709 Southwest Salmon Street
Portland, Oregon 97205

Sacramento

Church of Scientology
825 15th Street
Sacramento, California 95814

San Diego

Church of Scientology
701 "C" Street
San Diego, California 92101

San Francisco

Church of Scientology
83 McAllister Street
San Francisco, California 94102

San Jose

Church of Scientology
80 E. Rosemary
San Jose, California 95112

Santa Barbara

Church of Scientology
524 State Street
Santa Barbara, California 93101

Seattle

Church of Scientology
2004 Westlake Avenue
Seattle, Washington 98121

St. Louis

Church of Scientology
9510 Page Boulevard
St. Louis, Missouri 63132

Tampa

Church of Scientology
4809 North Armenia Avenue
Suite 215
Tampa, Florida 33603

Washington, DC

Founding Church of Scientology
2125 "S" Street NW
Washington, DC 20008

Canada

Edmonton

Church of Scientology
10349 82nd Avenue
Edmonton, Alberta
Canada T6E 1Z9

Kitchener

Church of Scientology
8 Water Street North
Kitchener, Ontario
Canada N2H 5A5

Montréal

Church of Scientology
4489 Papineau Street
Montréal, Québec
Canada H2H 1T7

Ottawa

Church of Scientology
150 Rideau Street, 2nd Floor
Ottawa, Ontario
Canada K1N 5X6

Quèbec

Church of Scientology
226 St-Joseph est
Québec, Québec
Canada G1K 3A9

Toronto

Church of Scientology
696 Yonge Street
Toronto, Ontario
Canada M4Y 2A7

Vancouver

Church of Scientology
401 West Hastings Street
Vancouver, British Columbia
Canada V6B 1L5

Winnipeg

Church of Scientology
Suite 125—388 Donald Street
Winnipeg, Manitoba
Canada R3B 2J4

United Kingdom

Birmingham

Church of Scientology
60/62 Constitution Hill
Birmingham
England B19 3JT

Brighton

Church of Scientology
Dukes Arcade, Top Floor
Dukes Street
Brighton, Sussex
England

East Grinstead

Saint Hill Foundation
Saint Hill Manor
East Grinstead, West Sussex
England RH19 4JY

Advanced Organization Saint Hill
Saint Hill Manor
East Grinstead, West Sussex
England RH19 4JY

Edinburgh

Hubbard Academy of Personal Independence
20 Southbridge
Edinburgh, Scotland EH1 1LL

London

Church of Scientology
68 Tottenham Court Road
London, England W1P 0BB

Manchester

Church of Scientology
258 Deansgate
Manchester, England M3 4BG

Plymouth

Church of Scientology
41 Ebrington Street
Plymouth, Devon
England PL4 9AA

Sunderland

Church of Scientology
51 Fawcett Street
Sunderland, Tyne and Wear
England SR1 1RS

Austria

Vienna

Church of Scientology
Schottenfeldgasse 13–15
1070 Vienna, Austria

Vienna South

Church of Scientology
Celebrity Centre VNA
Senefelderg. 12
A-1100 Vienna, Austria

Belgium

Brussels

Church of Scientology
45A, rue de l'Ecuyer
1000 Bruxelles, Belgium

Denmark

Aarhus

Church of Scientology
Guldsmedegade 17, 2
8000 Aarhus C, Denmark

Copenhagen

Church of Scientology
Vesterbrogade 66
1620 Copenhagen V, Denmark

Church of Scientology
Advanced Organization Saint Hill
for Europe and Africa
Jernbanegade 6
1608 Copenhagen V, Denmark

France

Angers

Church of Scientology
10–12, rue Max Richard
49000 Angers, France

Clermont-Ferrand

Church of Scientology
2 Pte rue Giscard de la Tour Fondue
63000 Clermont-Ferrand, France

Lyon

Church of Scientology
3, place des Capucins
69001 Lyon, France

Paris

Church of Scientology
65, rue de Dunkerque
75009 Paris, France

Church of Scientology
Celebrity Centre Paris
69, rue Legendre
75017 Paris, France

St. Etienne

Church of Scientology
24, rue Marengo
42000 St. Etienne, France

Germany

Berlin

Church of Scientology e.V.
Sponholzstrasse 51/52
1000 Berlin 41, Germany

Düsseldorf

Church of Scientology
Friedrichstrasse 28
4000 Düsseldorf, West Germany

Church of Scientology
Celebrity Centre Düsseldorf
Grupellostr. 28
4000 Düsseldorf, West Germany

Frankfurt

Church of Scientology
Darmstadter Landstrasse 213
6000 Frankfurt 70, West Germany

Hamburg

Church of Scientology e.V.
Steindamm 63
2000 Hamburg 1, West Germany

Church of Scientology
Celebrity Centre Hamburg
Mönckebergstrasse 5/IV
2000 Hamburg 1
West Germany

Hanover

Church of Scientology
Hubertusstrasse 2
D-3000 Hannover 1, West Germany

Munich

Church of Scientology e.V.
Beichstrasse 12
D-8000 München 40, West Germany

Stuttgart

Church of Scientology
Hirschstrasse 27
7000 Stuttgart, West Germany

Israel

Tel Aviv

Scientology and Dianetics College
7 Salomon Street
Tel Aviv 66023, Israel

Italy

Brescia

Church of Scientology
Dei Tre Laghi
Via Fratelli Bronzetti N. 20
25125 Brescia, Italy

Milano

Church of Scientology
Via Abetone, 10
20137 Milano, Italy

Monza

Church of Scientology
Via Cavour, 5
20052 Monza, Italy

Novara

Church of Scientology
Corso Cavallotti No. 7
28100 Novara, Italy

Nuoro

Church of Scientology
Via G. Deledda, 43
08100 Nuoro, Italy

Padua

Church of Scientology
Via Mameli 1/5
35131 Padova, Italy

Pordenone

Church of Scientology
Via Montereale, 10/C
33170 Pordenone, Italy

Rome

Church of Scientology
Via di San Vito, 11
00185 Roma, Italy

Turin

Church of Scientology
Via Guarini, 4
10121 Torino, Italy

Verona

Church of Scientology
Vicolo Chiodo No. 4/A
37121 Verona, Italy

Netherlands

Amsterdam

Church of Scientology
Nieuwe Zijds Voorburgwal 271
1012 RL Amsterdam, Netherlands

Norway

Oslo

Church of Scientology
Storgata 9
0155 Oslo 1, Norway

Portugal

Lisbon

Instituto de Dianética
Rua Actor Taborda 39–4°
1000 Lisboa, Portugal

Spain

Barcelona

Dianética
Calle Pau Claris 85, Principal 1ª
08010 Barcelona, Spain

Madrid

Asociación Civil de Dianética
Montera 20, Piso 1° DCHA
28013 Madrid, Spain

Sweden

Göteborg

Church of Scientology
Odinsgatan 8
411 03 Göteborg, Sweden

Malmö
Church of Scientology
Simrishamnsgatan 10
21423 Malmö, Sweden

Stockholm
Church of Scientology
Kammakargatan 46
S-111 60 Stockholm, Sweden

Switzerland

Basel
Church of Scientology
Herrengrabenweg 56
4054 Basel, Switzerland

Bern
Church of Scientology
Schulhausgasse 12
3113 Rubigen
Bern, Switzerland

Geneva
Church of Scientology
9 Route de Saint-Julien
1227 Carouge
Genève, Switzerland

Lausanne
Church of Scientology
10, rue de la Madeleine
1003 Lausanne, Switzerland

Zürich
Church of Scientology
Badenerstrasse 294
CH-8004 Zürich, Switzerland

Australia

Adelaide
Church of Scientology
24 Waymouth Street
Adelaide, South Australia 5000
Australia

Brisbane
Church of Scientology
2nd Floor, 106 Edward Street
Brisbane, Queensland 4000
Australia

Canberra
Church of Scientology
Suite 16, 108 Bunda Street
Canberra Civic
A.C.T. 2601, Australia

Melbourne
Church of Scientology
44 Russell Street
Melbourne, Victoria 3000
Australia

Perth
Church of Scientology
39–41 King Street
Perth, Western Australia 6000
Australia

Sydney
Church of Scientology
201 Castlereagh Street
Sydney, New South Wales 2000
Australia

Church of Scientology
Advanced Organization Saint Hill
Australia, New Zealand and
Oceania
19–37 Greek Street
Glebe, New South Wales 2037
Australia

Japan

Tokyo
Scientology Organization
101 Toyomi Nishi Gotanda Heights
2-13-5 Nishi Gotanda
Shinagawa-Ku
Tokyo, Japan 141

New Zealand

Auckland
Church of Scientology
32 Lorne Street
Auckland 1, New Zealand

Africa

Bulawayo
Church of Scientology
74 Abercorn Street
Bulawayo, Zimbabwe

Cape Town
Church of Scientology
5 Beckham Street
Gardens
Cape Town 8001, South Africa

Durban
Church of Scientology
57 College Lane
Durban 4001, South Africa

Harare
Church of Scientology
First Floor State Lottery Building
P.O. Box 3524
Corner Speke Avenue and
Julius Nyerere Way
Harare, Zimbabwe

Johannesburg
Church of Scientology
Security Building, 2nd Floor
95 Commissioner Street
Johannesburg 2001, South Africa

Church of Scientology
101 Huntford Building
40 Hunter Street
Cnr. Hunter & Fortesque Roads
Yeoville 2198
Johannesburg, South Africa

Port Elizabeth
Church of Scientology
2 St. Christopher
27 Westbourne Road
Central
Port Elizabeth 6001, South Africa

Pretoria
Church of Scientology
1st Floor City Centre
272 Pretorius Street
Pretoria 0002, South Africa

Latin America

Colombia

Bogotá
Centro Cultural de Dianética
Carrera 19 No. 39–55
Apartado Aereo 92419
Bogotá, D.E. Colombia

Mexico

Estado de México
Instituto Technologico de
Dianética, A.C.
Londres 38, 5th Floor
Col. Juarez, México D.F.

Guadalajara
Organización Cultural Dianética de
Guadalajara, A.C.
Av. Lopez Mateos Nte. 329
Sector Hidalgo
Guadalajara, Jalisco, México

Mexico City
Asociación Cultural Dianética, A.C.
Hermes No. 46
Colonia Crédito Constructor
03940 México 19, D.F.

Instituto de Filosofia Aplicada, A.C.
Durango #105
Colonia Roma
06700 México D.F.

Instituto de Filosofia Aplicada, A.C.
Plaza Rio de Janeiro No. 52
Colonia Roma
06700 México D.F.

Organización, Desarrollo y Dianética, A.C.
Providencia 1000
Colonia Del Valle
C.P. 03100 México D.F.

Centro de Dianética Polanco
Insurgentes Sur 536, 1er piso Esq. Nogales
Colonia Roma Sur C.P.
06700 México D.F.

Venezuela

Valencia

Asociación Cultural Dianética de Venezuela, A.C.
Ave. 101 No. 150–23
Urbanizacion La Alegria
Apartado Postal 833
Valencia, Venezuela

To obtain any books or cassettes by L. Ron Hubbard which are not available at your local organization, contact any of the following publishers:

Bridge Publications, Inc.
4751 Fountain Avenue
Los Angeles, California 90029

Continental Publications Liaison Office
696 Yonge Street
Toronto, Ontario
Canada M4Y 2A7

NEW ERA Publications International, ApS
Store Kongensgade 55
1264 Copenhagen K, Denmark

Era Dinámica Editores, S.A. de C.V.
Alabama 105
Colonia Nápoles
C.P. 03810 México D.F.

NEW ERA Publications, Ltd.
78 Holmethorpe Avenue
Redhill, Surrey RH1 2NL
United Kingdom

N.E. Publications Australia Pty. Ltd.
2 Verona Street
Paddington, New South Wales 2021
Australia

Continental Publications Pty. Ltd.
P.O. Box 27080
Benrose 2011
South Africa

NEW ERA Publications Italia Srl
Via L.G. Columella, 12
20128 Milano, Italy

NEW ERA Publications GmbH
Otto—Hahn—Strasse 25
6072 Dreieich 1, Germany

NEW ERA Publications France
111, Boulevard de Magenta
75010 Paris, France

New Era Publications España, S.A.
C/De la Paz, 4/1° dcha
28012 Madrid, Spain

New Era Japan
5-4-5-803 Nishi Gotanda
Shinagawa-Ku
Tokyo, Japan 141